A Full Answer to the Conduct of the Allies

A FULL
ANSWER
TO THE
Conduct of the Allies:

To which is added, some

OBSERVATIONS
ON THE
REMARKS on the Barrier Treaty.

By the same AUTHOR.

LONDON:

Printed in the Year MDCCXII.

[Price One Shilling.]

A FULL
ANSWER
TO THE
CONDUCT, &c.

HOW much the Design of this *Pamphlet* is owing to the miserable Necessity of State-Policy, may be best prov'd, by considering the Purpose it is writ to serve, and by the Protection it receives from those, who wou'd not, I believe, upon any other Reason, give it countenance. Whilst I am speaking of this, I cannot forget a lively Instance of such a kind of miserable Policy in those Mariners, who, when their Vessel strikes on a Rock, forgetting their common Safety, have recourse to some extraordinary and mistaken Means; the Advice, perhaps, of a few hardy Persons among them, who, out of a Caprice of gratifying their own Judgment, or, more probably, with too near a regard for their own private Safety, occasion the ruin of themſelves, and all that are embark'd with them. How near a ſituation is there in the infamous Conduct of thoſe, who let out their Pens to hire, and for the vile conſideration of Pay, write in oppoſition to all Truth and Honeſty, nay, even to their own Conſciences; there is much more to be ſaid for thoſe, who only take a ſcandalous Penſion to be ſilent.

It was long before this Book fell into my Hands, and longer before I form'd a Reſolution to ſpend any Time about it, till on a ſecond or third reading every Line preſented me with a freſh Inſtance of Aggravation. As to the Author, I eſteem it needleſs to enquire after him, ſince Libels of this kind, uſually, receive their *Grand Maſter-Strokes* from thoſe to whoſe Intereſt and Service they are calculated and aſſign'd. Now is it not matter of Wonder and Reflection, that there ſhould be thoſe, who will countenance an ill Thing, for the good they are to receive by it. These are what I call *The miſerable Neceſſities of State-Policy*, where to ſupport the Meaſures of a Few, a whole Nation ſhall be expos'd to Danger and Ruin. And it is poſſible ſometimes a good Man may be ſpirited away by their inchanting Devices, but that is only for a Time, for ſuch will, of courſe, find out the Deceit, and deſert thoſe by whom they have been drawn in to act wrong, thro' an implicite overſight, and this with the utmoſt Reflection of Hatred and Contempt. For as ſuch *Politicks*, generally require the moſt violent Meaſures to ſupport them, ſo their Courſe is ſeldom long, and generally terminates by ſome ſudden and unexpected Event.

I come now to our **Conducter**, whoſe Arguments, I confeſs, I cannot but admire; there appears in them throughout, ſuch a wonderful and peculiar Spirit of Cunning, as can be equall'd by nothing but a Falſhood as notorious: And it may, with

with very little Circumſpection, be obſerv'd, how cloſe he follows his Blow, and how little regard he has to Truth, when he handles any particular Point, where the Reputation of his Friends ſeems moſt at Stake, and while he is only pretending to write for the Intereſt of his Country, is betraying the Honour of it to a baſe Degree; from whence, it is probable, he has borrow'd his excellent Maxims of treating crown'd Heads, abuſing thoſe in Alliance with us, and at the ſame Time extolling our Enemies, and making way for our being impos'd upon. A Proceeding ſo very new and extraordinary, that, I confeſs, I am at a loſs what Name to give it.

What ſhall be done to the Man whom the King honours? was ſaid of old; ſo by a Parity of Words, What ſhall be ſaid to the Man, that vilifies and expoſes his Country, whoſe chief Buſineſs, it ſeems, to repreſent Her in a languiſhing and ruin'd Condition? And what Effect can it have, but to afford our Enemies the Advantage? To render us deſpicable Abroad, and inſecure at Home? And to remove all Obſtacles in his Power, out of the Way of Peace; ſuch a Peace as his Friends are Treating, and he Writing for. What is this, but to give our Enemies a Handle to treat us with Barbarity and Inſolence; the Effect of which, I think, they have given us a very melancholly Inſtance of already; and I doubt not but we ſhall taſte more of their innate Love and Goodneſs to us hereafter, according as they receive Encouragement from the **Conductor**, and his Friends: And, it has been found, by former Experience, that a very ſmall Encouragement will ſerve turn, when, in breach of all that is Solemn and Religious, they put on us the greateſt Indignities that ever any Nation ſuffer'd, by which our Honour was leſſen'd and impair'd, and the Standard of it ſcarce valuable in any Nation in *Europe*, till the Succeſſes of this

 Reign,

Reign, (under the Conduct and Management of those, who have been treated accordingly) rais'd it again to its intrinsick Value: And do's he now say, we might with Honour and Safety have declin'd entering into the present War? Cou'd we sit down with the scandalous Affront put on us, in proclaiming the *Pretender*? or, rather, shou'd we not resolve never to forget it, but make a Reprizal, now it is in our Power, by imposing something as mortifying on the Enemy? If I may be allow'd to term the King of *France* so? Do we not bleed for it to this Day? And is it any more than a Prelude to the scandalous Affront lately put on Her Majesty, and to all the Indignities he shall think fit to impose on us hereafter, even the *Pretender* himself, when an occasion presents, if we leave no better Bulwarks than this **Conducter**, and his Friends? *And this*, he says, *the* French King *had as much Reason to do, as we to impose a King upon* Spain. The World may see that he do's not desire to make much difference between the *Pretender*'s Title to the Crown of *England*, and that of the House of *Austria* to the *Spanish Monarchy*; and no doubt but he'll have a Reason ready to back this *Traiterous Inuendo*, when Opportunity requires: But to put an end to this Point, we will not dispute, which had most Reason to do, but which had least Reason to suffer what was done. It was sufficient to justifie, past all Exception, our Conduct of entering, as Principals, into the present War, and instead of not being so much concern'd as our Neighbours, to prove that we were a great deal more, and even most of all: The *Dutch* fought to enlarge their Frontier, the *Emperor* for the Right of the House of *Austria*, and *Others* upon the different Views of Interest; but we enter'd into the War to preserve what we had; to secure our selves against Popery, and the Friends of it, and a very great Point too, if we gain'd it, contrary to the

ridicu-

ridiculous Similitude *of the House on Fire*, where he says— *The Neighbours run with Buckets to quench it; but the Owner is sure to be undone first, and it is not impossible that Those at the next Door may escape by a Shower from Heaven, the Stillness of the Weather, or some other favourable Accident.* Was there ever such a wretched and silly Position? What do's it but allow that We must have trusted meerly to a Possibility for Our Salvation? which they that rely on deserve to smart for, as the Reward of so much Folly. I believe, shou'd One endeavour to persuade a Person, when a Fire is next Door to him, that he need not stir, for it may *Possibly* fall a Raining, or some *Favourable Accident* may happen to preserve his Goods, that such a One wou'd be apt to compliment you with his Excuse: And truly, he that wou'd not come out of the Fire to hear This, deserves to be burnt. But, indeed, it is consonant to the Miracle that must have sav'd Us, had We stood still till the *Dutch* had been destroy'd before our Faces, and not acted with that great Vigour and Harmony which the Case requir'd; where we shou'd only have experienc'd the miserable Curtesie of *Polyphemus* to *Ulysses*, of being reserv'd to be last devour'd.

His *Encomium*, and the wrested Comparison of a Civil War, bears much the same Analogy to Reason and good Sense; for when we shall once be convinc'd where Those People dwell, who are so fond of the Inconvenience and Ravages of an Army, that They wou'd not pay a little Money to be rid of Their good Company; I shall grant this Conducter to have more Reason of his Side than I thought he had: But so miserably fond is he, of saying any thing, that he thinks may make for his *Purpose*, that he very often forgets himself.

His admirable Instance of the *Dutch* Wars, in the Reign of King *Charles* the Second, (which, indeed, he might have term'd a Civil War too, if Quarelling with our Friends be so) is very moving: *This*, he says, *was begun, and carried on, under a very corrupt Administration, and much to the dishonour of the Crown*, (as all *Dutch* Wars will be) *kept the King poor and needy, by discontinuing, or discontenting his Parliament, when he most needed their Assistance, but neither left any Debt upon the Nation, nor carried any Money out of it.*

No, but the Expence of Three or Four Millions then, had sav'd Us a Hundred since; and I dare engage it was such another Set of Principles as now reign, that advis'd the King to that Unreasonable and Unnatural War, who concur'd with him in acting contrary to the Interest of his Country: But the Parliament, it may be remember'd, wou'd never be wrought upon to give in to such destructive Measures; nor have we yet retriev'd that false Step, of weakning our selves and the *Dutch* by a kind of intestine War, Voted meerly to humour those, who were the Friends of *France*, and acted in a Parallel with too many at this Juncture.

The Revolution is one of the next things he has a fling at; and here he tells us, *That a general War broke out, wherein several Princes join'd in Alliance against* France, *to check the Ambitious Designs of that Monarch; and here the* Emperor; *the* Dutch, *and* English, *were Principals. And that the Ground of this War as to the Parts we had in it, was to make* France *acknowledge King* William, *and to recover* Hudsons-Bay. It is certain that these Two Points were chiefly insisted on, but the War in general, was to check the Ambition of *France*, who by unheard of Breaches of Faith, had born a heavy Hand over all his Neighbours. As an Instance of it, the *French* King had begun a War, by invading the Empire just before the Revolution; which might have prevented the Success of it, and thereby the more endanger'd the Liberty of *Europe*. Nor is it true, *that the Sea was neglected*, for, I think, during much the greatest part of that War, which began in 1689, we were en-

tirely

tirely Masters of the Sea, by our Victory in 1692, which was only 3 Years after it broke out; so that for 7 Years in 10 we carried the *Broom*.

And for any neglect of our Sea-Affairs, otherwise, I believe, I may, in few Words, prove that all the Princes from the Conquest, never made so remarkable an Improvement to our Naval, strength as King *William*. He shou'd have been told, if he did not know, what Havock the *Dutch* had made of our Shipping in King *Charles* the Second's Reign, and that his Successor King *James* the Second, had not in his whole Navy, fitted out to Defeat the design'd Invasion by the Prince of *Orange*, One individual Ship, of the First or Second Rank, which all lay neglected, and meer Skeletons of former Services, at their Moorings. These, this abus'd Prince, repair'd at an immense Charge, and brought them to their pristine Magnificence. Let us add to this, the Glory of re-establishing the value of our Coin, and, I think, these are Two Things the Friends of *France* ought never to forgive him. To this Assertion, the **Conducter** adds, *That the greatest part of Six Millions was Annually employ'd to enlarge a* Dutch-*Frontier, because the King was a General, and not an Admiral; and tho' King of* England, *a Native of* Holland. This is no more than a Scandalous Assertion, and not justified by the appearance of any matter of Fact; for what I have said before, proves us clearly out of danger as to the Sea, and therefore that it remain'd but a necessary Consequence, to make all possible Efforts against *France* on the side of *Flanders*, and all that we did make, prov'd little enough, partly thro' the ill Treatment the King receiv'd at Home, and partly thro' a bad Trade, and ill Credit; nor did the Service after all, employ *the greatest part of Six Millions*, as may be seen by the Estimates laid before the Parliament every Sessions. And coming to the End of the War, he says, *That after the loss of an Hundred Thou-*

sand

sand Men, and a Debt of Six Millions remaining, a Peace was concluded with great Advantages to the Empire and Holland, *but none at all to Us.* Whether, (but as a Reflection on the late King, as he designs it, this ought not to have been charg'd on the Perfidy of the King of *France*, who made Peace at that Time only with design to break it; who, having private Assurances of the ill State of the Health of the King of *Spain*, deceiv'd the Allies by false Terms of Peace, to get into quiet Possession of the *Spanish-Netherlands*, which, if he had not effected by a special Instance of Treachery, he must have won by the Sword, tho' his Grandson had succeeded to the Throne. Neither cou'd I ever perceive the great Advantages of this Peace, either to the *Empire* or *Holland*. We all know the Emperor was abandon'd, and left to accept such Terms as were allotted him, nor cou'd we be brought to listen to his Representations, tho' never so pressing, which, if we had done, as is much the Case now, 'tis very probable, we had not been troubled with this Second War. And besides, the former War having been unsuccessful, it will not be easily conceiv'd, what Advantages any, in the Grand-Alliance, cou'd reap by it; and even those that were Stipulated for the *Empire* and *Holland*, it is well known were never Executed.

To shew his Contempt of the *Monied Interest*, he tells you, *that in this War began the Custom of borrowing Millions upon Funds of Interest*, the true Reason of which he adds was for *the Security of a new Prince, not firmly settled on the Throne.* This it is known was occasion'd by a Set of Men in P——t, whose Ambition it was to affront the King, and cramp Him in His Subsidies, for which Reason They wou'd never be brought to think of any Thing like an Excise, which Method however has been taken up since, and those very Persons the most forward in Voting it; which had they done at First the Nation had not been charg'd with so many heavy Debts. Nor

after

after all, is there any Thing in this Method, but that all the Nations engag'd in these Wars have put in practice, as well as Our selves, and lie under the same Engagements for Money.

I shou'd be glad to get over some Assertions that lie in my Way, that I might come to Matters of Fact; but as there are many of 'em, so Ridiculous, False, and Absurd, it will appear of some Service to give a Check to Them; and chiefest of which he lays down under Three distinct Heads. First, *That against all manner of Prudence and Common Sense, We engag'd in this War as Principals, when We ought to have Acted only as* Auxiliaries. Which, I think, I have given sufficient Reasons to confute already; besides, its being contrary to the Sense of all the Parliaments, since the War began, the constrant, and repeated Sense of Her Majesty and all Her Allies; nay, even of the Present P———t, a Year ago, who, in Their Representation, *Speak of the absolute Necessity of Carrying on the War.* Nor is it only contrary to the Sense of the Present P———t, but, I think, of the Present M———y too, no long Time ago. The D. of *M———h* was again sent to Command the Army in *Flanders*, notwithstanding the Clamours against Him since. This makes it plain, that People may fluctuate in their Opinions, according as their *Purpose* requires; for what he has been charg'd with since, has not been committed since, and might as well have been laid to his Charge, before the last Campagne, as now: They cannot deny the Knowledge of it I suppose, and it wou'd not be believ'd if they did; therefore it must be affirm'd, that out of Choice, in their own Sense. They put a G——l at the Head of the Army, that had cheated his Country, and wrong'd the Soldiers; and was like to do the same again, because the Matters in Dispute were Grand-Perquisites, which he had taken all the War: And, to do them this Justice, I believe all the Generals in *Europe* ever did the like, tho' perhaps with some Difference in the Incidents. Now the Use I make of this, is only to prove that the Sense of some People has greatly chang'd in a Twelve-months Time, and especially since Mr. *P——r*'s Journey to *PARIS*. There was then some new Steps to be taken, and even the very Scriblers of the Party, that had been kept in Ignorance before, began now to catch at the new Sentiments of their Masters, as may be seen by many scandalous Pamphlets after that memorable Time, and especially that before me, which led the Van; and now they let go their Hold of the late M———y, and began to fasten on Our Allies, for their Malice in blackening the former, wou'd not carry the Point far enough: There must be a Quarrel pick'd with the *Dutch*, in particular, and the D. of *M——b* first be sacrific'd to humour it; neither the Zeal, or the Vigour of the One, nor the Services of the Other, can skreen them; it is sufficient that they stood in the Way of bringing a very material *Purpose* to bear; and their Treatment of them and the rest of the Confederates, added something very Sanguine to the Complexion of Peace, and was the True Reason why the Conduct comes to say, *That it was against all Manner of Prudence or Common Reason, that We Engag'd in the War; and that Her Majesty, by the Grand Alliance, is not oblig'd to demand the Restitution of* Spain.

The QUEEN's Declaration for War, he tells us, *does not take Notice of the Duke of* Anjou's *Succession to that Monarchy, as a Subject of Quarrel*; and has given Us a good Part of that Declaration in his Libel. The Grand Design of which being to instill into the Nation a corrupt Notion of Peace, and the Necessity of it, he labours with great Industry to remove all Scruples that may arise in honest Minds, in relation to it. And if he can but persuade them *that the War, in itself, was wrong begun; that the Grand Alliance, does not oblige Us to insist on Re-*

stitution

stitution of Spain, *and that the Allies having acted basely by us, it is no Dishonour to abandon them:* What Difficulty ought we to make of compelling them to make Peace on our own Methods, without *Spain*, and the *Indies*. Is not this a rare Scheme, contriv'd to break the Grand-Alliance, and for the same Reasons to undermine the Revolution, which I presume, is to be the Conducters next Work, when he has fully carried this preliminary Point toward it. And this, perhaps, is the meaning of that Blunt Intimation he gives us, *that the Necessities of the Nation may require them to alter the Succession.* And this, tho' he says he has explain'd in a latter Edition, yet the Hint remains good. Now I wou'd have the Author let us know what kind of Reason, or Necessity it can be, that shou'd make us alter the Succession, (even tho', as he says, in future Ages) and whether any Necessity, according to his beloved Doctrine, can give the *Legislature* a Power to alter the Succession, which our Representatives are chosen to preserve, but not destroy: But of this hereafter.

To prove that *England*, by all Her Treaties, is oblig'd to insist on the Restitution of the *Spanish* Monarchy, the best way will be to look into the Treaties themselves, where we shall expresly find our selves under that Obligation. And can it be said, That these Treaties are not as binding as the Grand Alliance; I am sure there is one Reason they shou'd be more; They were made upon a great deal more Deliberation, nor can these Treaties be call'd, *the Contrivance of a Faction*, that were transacted in the Second Year of the War, when the M——y was in the Hands of such as were zealously affected to the Church; and the P——t of the same Complexion. So that our Conducter was not in any great Concern for the Reputation of his Friends, when he endeavours to weaken the Authority of Treaties which were concluded under

their

their auspicious Conduct; of which no body at that Time pretended to complain, but were pleas'd with the Restoration of Credit; the Successes of the War, and the wise and frugal Management of the Treasury.

I hope the Conducter will allow, that no Treaties were ever better consider'd than those made with France and Savoy, at that time; where the Restitution of the *Spanish* Monarchy is stipulated past all manner of Contradiction. But to put the Matter farther out of dispute, it is easy to prove, that the Restitution of *Spain*, and the *Indies*, to the House of *Austria*, is not a new Demand, started since the Grand-Alliance, as it is pretended, but was the First separate Article in the former Alliance of 1689, where the States and we engage, *That in Case the King of* Spain, (Chap. 2.) *shou'd dye without Issue, they will with all their Forces assist his Sacred Imperial Majesty, or his Heirs, in taking the Succession of the* Spa*nish Monarchy lawfully belonging to that House.* Is not this a very insolent Charge then of the Conducter, that it is the Work of a late Faction? a new Incident; to insist on the Restitution of *Spain*, when the Allies oblig'd themselves to it about a Dozen Years before, and even at the time of the Revolution; and which do's and will appear to have been the constant Sense of all the *Allies*, and of every Body else, till the Contradiction of it has been taken up, as an Expedient to serve a particular End.

And, is it not plain, That the *First Grand-Alliance* is the original Ground of our Quarrel, the Source of all we have been endeavouring at since. Did our being in more danger, alter the necessity of our Engagements with our Allies, with all the benefit of the *Partition-Treaty* thrown into the Scale? What can the Arguments made use of by the Conducter, tend to, but utterly to overturn the *Grand-Aliance*, which is the main Pillar and Sup-

port

port of the *Revolution*, and will, in all probability, draw along with it the subversion of it.

He tells us, *We had no Quarrel with* France, *but his owning the* Pretender, *which might easily have been made up, for the* French *Court declar'd, That they did not acknowledge the* Pretender, *but only gave him the Title of* King, *which was allow'd to* Augustus, *by the King of* Sweden. What an utter Falshood is this? King *Augustus* was allow'd, by the Treaty, to stile himself King, but not King of *Poland*; whereas the *Pretender* was not simply stiled King *James*, but *His Britannick Majesty*, and *King of Great Britain*; and this, I think, no body disputes, that read, at that Time, the *Paris-Gazettes*, and other publick News-Papers. But our Conducter's Purpose requir'd to Shuffle in this Equivocation; and to give it a little colouring to help it out, he translates the VIIIth Article in such a manner, as to make the World think that nothing else was meant on the part of *England*, but to insist on satisfaction for this great Affront. The Sense of which Article plainly covenants for the Security of His Majesty's Kingdoms, and Commerce, as well as that of the *States General*; and in the Article just before this, we have it thus: *For obtaining satisfaction for the Emperor, and the aforesaid Security for his* Britannick *Majesty, and the* States.

The same Article says, That no Peace shall be made without Security; *That the* French *shall never get into the possession of the* Spanish West-Indies, *nor be permitted to sail thither on any account of Traffick, directly nor indirectly, on any Pretence whatever.* Now, pray let this Author tell us, how, or which way we shall be secure of this, if *Spain* be left to the House of *Bourbon*? Is not *France*, at this Time, in possession of the *West Indies*, and have they not actually Settlements there at *Lima*, and other Places, and can we believe they will easily quit them? or, Have they promis'd such a Thing to our Negotiators

gotiators of Peace? if they have not, I think we cannot make Peace with them, upon the Terms impos'd. And here I must make an Observation by the way, That whoever shall compare the late Offers of *France*, with any manner of circumspection, to the *Conduct of the Allies*, will find how critically they are built upon the Author's Arguments, and even the very Words, in some Places, interwove in the same artful manner, to shadow the Imperfections. That I think it is plain, the *Conduct* had been well read over in *France*, before they concluded on their *Proposals*.

Next, I wou'd fain know, what Security they can ever propose, *that* France *and* Spain *shall never be united?* unless giving it wholly out of their Power, or how either we or our Allies can be safe, when the exorbitant Power of *France*, founded on such destructive Maxims, shall be strengthen'd by the Riches of the *Indies*? where, besides what he enjoys already, he has Treaties with his Grandson, for much larger Encroachments.

What therefore can be meant by saying, *That the Allies demand no more for the Emperor, than a just and reasonable satisfaction*. And is it any more than just and reasonable satisfaction, that he shou'd have those Dominions which the King of *France* has solemnly renounc'd for himself, and his Descendants, besides the undoubted Right thereto of the House of *Austria*, or shall it, by the same Rule, be call'd any more than a reasonable Satisfaction to us, that a strict regard be had to putting it out of his Power before we make Peace, ever to throw in the *Pretender* upon us? which Experience may sufficiently convince us, will never be the Effect of *His Most Christian Majesty*'s Conscience.

The next Point he finds necessary to support his Cavil by, (a Reason, which no doubt but he understands as well as he handles) is to persuade us,

That

That we have pursu'd the War in a wrong Method, and spent all our Vigour, where it wou'd least Answer our Ends; and made no Efforts where we might have weaken'd the common Enemy, and Enrich'd our selves. And again, That we suffer'd each of our Allies to break every Article of those Treaties and Agreements, by which They were bound, to lay all the burthen upon us. Now the Method the War has been pursu'd in, as well in the choice of it, as in the Event, must be attributed to general Councils of War, unanimously agreed among all the Allies: No positive Directions is I presume, meant to proceed from hence, as an unreasonable charge upon the late M——y; nor can it be thought the result of a secret Agreement between our G—l and the *Dutch*, to make way for their Advantage. Well then, where shall I fix this Authors meaning, *that we might best have weaken'd the Enemy?* Since he is not so honest to tell us; which he might have easily done, and it wou'd have been very much to his Credit, as well as of Advantage in proving his Point. Or was he afraid to discover so rich a Secret, lest we shou'd yet make use of it to weaken the Interest of his Friends: No, I have a better Opinion of him; but that according to his usual Method, it was to raise a great deal of Dust about something, that has nothing in it: I must therefore run thro' the several Branches of the War, that I may be sure to hit the right Nail, which by the way, is giving himself and me more trouble, than there was absolutely occasion for.

To say therefore that we shou'd have push'd the War in *Spain*; *the Recovery of which was the chief thing we enter'd into the War for*, is a very mistaken Notion, if it be our Authors meaning. Let us but consider upon how unequal a Foot we must have manag'd an Offensive War in that Country in regard to the many conveniences the *French* wou'd have found to disappoint us; and the Reasons which wou'd not have been sufficient to convince the wrong Notion of a Set of Men at Home, might perhaps have had as little force on the Inclinations of our Allies, in persuading them to comply with Measures so very unlikely to succeed. We know the *Party* have more than once hinted at weakening our selves in *Flanders*, to make Efforts in *Spain*, but this was urg'd meerly as a Mark of their good Will to the D—e of *M———h*, who once gave them an Answer in the L—s House to this Point that stopt their Mouths. Suppose then, we had follow'd their Advice, and been inclin'd to send a Reinforcement of 20000 Men from *Flanders*; which way were they to be got thither? First they wou'd have prov'd an excessive Charge to Transport them thither; which we had no other way for, but an uncertain Passage by Sea from *England*, where what by the hazard of Storms, contrary Winds, Sickness, Desertion, and the danger of losing some Transports by the Enemies Privateers, or otherwise, these Men before they had arriv'd on the Spot for Service, wou'd have very probably been reduc'd to half their Number; and even those not fit for Service, till they had been sent into Quarters of Refreshment, where it was much, but by eating the Rich Fruits, the change of the Climate, and Drinking of the strong *Spanish* Wines, their Number had been a second time greatly diminish'd.

And again, this cou'd not have been done without Lessening our Army in *Flanders*, which the Enemy wou'd have made their Advantage of, by making a Detachment of half the Number serve, as an Equivalent for the War in *Spain*, and so gain a Superiority of 10000 Men out of 20000, or inproportion to the half of what we sent on every such occasion. And these they might have drawn from *Dauphine*, which might have been supply'd from the *Rhine*, or even from *Flanders*, by an easy, and very certain March;

which

which might have been done at a proper Season, and with little hazard, as we have often seen thro' the course of the War. Besides the Generals of the Enemy might have concerted their Measures accordingly, because they might have receiv'd Accounts to the very Day these Troops wou'd have reach'd them, and what Number, almost to a Man, they consisted of: Whereas, in our Case, the Generals cou'd have made no Advantage; they cou'd resolve on nothing, but to have lain under a tedious Expectation, waiting for Succours, of which they cou'd have no Accounts till they saw them; and even then cou'd have expected no immediate Service, and very probably the Season for the Campagne had been almost wasted. Their Transportation being not only hazardous and uncertain, attended with many unlucky Events, but likewise an excessive Charge, and always double to the Service it procures, because Provision is made for such a particular Number of Troops, when, as I have said, seldom above half their Number arrive compleat. Whereas the March of the Enemies Troops stands them in little or nothing and when they arrive, they are what they set out, and agree in Constitution with the Climate. Nor is is this all that might be said: I wou'd ask the **Conducter**, if we shou'd provide for an offensive War in *Spain*, how they must subsist? When the Country is hardly able to subsist it's own Inhabitants. Those Parts especially where our Armies Quarter. Of what then are we to form Magazines; if the growth of the Country affords barely enough for present necessity? And whence are they to be fetch'd? Why either from *Italy*, *England*, or the Coast of *Africk*; but then, as I have observ'd, the Transporting them thither is very hazardous and uncertain. And if even in *Flanders*, which is the finest Country in the Universe, to subsist an Army in, our Soldiers are sometimes driven to straits, by being at some distance from their Magazines, when the Roads are spoil'd in a bad Season; 'tis easy to guess what it must be in *Catalonia*, where to subsist only a very moderate Army is difficult enough. While the *French*, by the Contiguity of their Country, and the nearness of their Ports have the Advantage of supplying the Magazines of *Spain*; besides the Duke of *Anjou* possesses all those Provinces which are in Tranquility, and therefore capable if any are, of affording Relief for his Armies.

This I think is sufficient to prove, that *Spain* is not the Place where we shou'd have pursu'd the War; where even a Defensive One, with more Success than we cou'd well have hoped for, has prov'd difficult enough; and this by the way, is one Reason, why the *Dutch* have for these Three or Four Years past, sent no fresh Troops thither; but added their proportion elsewhere, as I shall shew anon.

But if this be the Case, it will be said, Why did we then begin this War at first? Or have not long since quitted it? Either of which Propositions may be easily answer'd. When we enter'd into the War, it was upon the most promising Suggestions that cou'd possibly be conceiv'd, that the *Spaniards* were ripe for a Revolt, cou'd we once get Footing, and tho' they did not answer our Expectations, yet when once we had Lodg'd our selves, it must have been a great Oversight to have quitted our Ground; and I think the wonderful struggles we have made there, have given the Enemy sufficient Charge and Trouble, and been often very fatal to their Affairs, and had not the Inconveniences I have spoke of; hinder'd us from sending necessary and timely Assistance, after any of our Successes, the War had been at End there long ago; which is a sufficient Argument against an offensive War in *Spain*, by weakening our Army in *Flanders*, which has always been the Cry, but is notoriously wrong. Besides when those Forces first Embark'd, as it was very difficult to determine at this distance, which way they might best answer the Good of the Common Cause, whether to Land in *Catalonia*, or give some Relief to the Duke of *Savoy*, who was at that time in need enough of it, it was left to the Determination of the Kings of *Portugal* and *Spain*, what Measures were to be taken; and after it had been thoroughly Debated in several Great Councils of War, it was resolv'd, at the Intercession of King *Charles* to Sail for *Catalonia*, who shew'd the many repeated Assurances he had receiv'd from the *Catalans* to Declare for him, if he were once in a condition to protect Them. And it was the rather agreed to, in regard of the desperate State of Affairs in *Italy*, where it was probable it wou'd give some Diversi- to the Enemy. Besides at this time, there was hardly an appearance of making so great an Impression in *Flanders*, much less cou'd we hope for a probability of penetrating into *France* on that side, as is become the Case now, and was sometime ago, or you had scarce had such humble Intreaties to be heard on the Subjects of Peace, and such Concessions made, notwithstanding, you had been in possession of the *Spanish* Monarchy, the *Indies* excepted. These were the Reasons for making Tryal of a War in *Spain*, and tho' it did not wholly answer our Expectations, it has been of consequence enough to deserve to be supported, and especially, after we had set Their King once among Them, when to have abandon'd him, or withdrawn our Troops, cou'd not have been done, but with the greatest Advantage to the Enemy, and the highest Dishonour to our selves and him; sufficient to have made the *Spaniards* for ever after contemn him, tho' we had obtain'd the Crown for him, which was not then disputed, but we must do by some *Method* or other, before the War shou'd cease.

Again, our keeping footing in *Catalonia*, and being Masters of *Barcelona*, as it keeps the Enemy,

 the

the *Spaniards* especially, in perpetual Alarms, so it gives Life and Spirit to our Friends, who, by this Situation, are encourag'd to act; and 'tis certain, the *Miquilets* do great service, whereas the Enemy are oblig'd to weaken their Troops on the Side of *Portugal*, which might have turn'd to a much greater advantage than we see has been made of it. However, it has oblig'd the Enemy to employ an Army much superior to ours, to watch our Motions, and alarms the Duke of *Anjou* with continual Distrusts of his Subjects, and to think himself safe in nothing but *French* Councils, and *French* Armies, which may have a better Effect, than, perhaps, we can yet foresee. Which Arguments, with many other of less Consequence, that might be brought, are sufficient to justifie the beginning of the War in *Spain*, and the carrying it on in the Method it has been, without enlarging the Scheme of War, which, instead of doing service to the common Cause, as I have shewn, wou'd render a double advantage to our Enemies.

Now, if to have carry'd the War on, on the *Rhine*, is the Method meant; which I hardly think it is, a few Words will easily convince us of the Improbability of making any advantage on that Side. It cannot be so much as thought that they cou'd be wanted there to act on the defensive; and all the World is convinc'd, that the Empire, on that Side, have no One Thing necessary for an offensive War; neither Money, Magazines, Amunition, *&c.* and, supposing they had, to what purpose wou'd it be, if the Army did not take the Field betimes, which is a Thing never to be hoped on the *Rhine*; and this is, doubtless, the chief Reason that the Emperor, for some Years past, sent such a number of Troops from thence to *Flanders*, where they might act to most advantage, and where nothing was like to be wanting to render them serviceable in the highest manner.

Then,

Then, lest another Thing shou'd be said, That they might clear their Way to the *Moselle* (on which Side *France* is indeed most expos'd;) and there have *pursu'd the right Method.* I think it were easie to answer, That that Experiment has been made already, when the Duke of *M*——— by an incredible Success, had, in a few Weeks, drawn the Seat of the War from the *Danube* to the *Rhine*, and thence to the *Moselle:* He march'd the next Campagne with a glorious Army thither, where had not the Reasons I have given before, been found too true, 'tis probable the War had soon been ended. Here he oblig'd the *French* General to retire before him, and to leave him at liberty to besiege *Saar-Lewis*, but, when he had done, he found the Imperial General very far from being able to answer any of his Engagements on which the Measures for pushing the War on that Side had been concerted; which together with the necessity of his presence in *Flanders*, oblig'd him to march back, and to make no more unhappy Experiments where the Promises of the Empire were not to be relied on.

And it is from hence, very probable, that shou'd a Project have been started for his marching to *Savoy*, which was once his Grace's Thoughts, and to have attack'd *France* on that side, had this been liable to any more success; and wou'd not the *Party* have exclaim'd, as they did on his march to the *Danube*, that he was run away with the Army? And what is ever to be hoped, where the Snows, and bad Season, leave not above Two Months good to make the Campagne, and the *French* might have drawn what Strength they pleas'd from *Flanders*, or the *Rhine*, with half the ease to have oppos'd us? Or, had the *Scotch-Expedition* happen'd in that Interval, as it is within the compass of the same Time, what Clamours wou'd the restless Spirit of the Duke's Enemies have rais'd against him, as if he had betray'd, and sold us to the Enemy. But I shall say no more of this, as hardly deserving notice, but that the **Conducter's** cunning Assertions draw One into it, and that he may have no Recess, or Assylum to fly to for the future.

But quoting his Assertion again, I find there is a Sting in the Tail of it; *where we might most have weaken'd the common Enemy, and* ENRICHED OUR SELVES. By this, I begin to think, we have all this while misunderstood him; and that we shou'd have carried the War into the *Spanish-West Indies*, if we had pursu'd the right Method; a wonderful Project indeed: But till the **Conducter**, and his Friends give us a better Account of the *Canada-Expedition*, which, I presume, was founded on this noble Scheme; I must beg his pardon for approving of burying Men and Money, at that rate; it looks, I must tell him, a little too much like a Castle in the Air: But I hear nothing said of it, the G——l has been rewarded for losing our Ships and Men, more than another wou'd have been, who had come home with Spoil and Conquest; a very pretty way *of enriching our selves*, and carrying on the War in a right Method, while for want of such a Squadron, we suffer'd our Allies, and our Selves to be plunder'd at *Brazil*: And this, I suppose, is what the **Conducter** means by *conquering something for our Selves*; but the Experiment is over, and, I hope, we shall make no more of them at so dear a rate.

Flanders therefore is the Place where we have push'd the War in the wrong Place; *France* being cover'd by so formidable a Barrier on that Side. The **Conducter**, as I observ'd before, shou'd have shewn us a better Place to lay the Stress of the War, than in *Flanders*, and then I wou'd have answer'd him, That, 'tis probable, be where it will, it might not have met with half the Success it has done there; and tho' it might be wrong at first, it has certainly answer'd beyond our Expectations, and is right now: Had

I not

I not shew'd that all Places had been Try'd, or at least, prudently and deliberately consider'd in the most consumate Councils of War; the unanimous consent of the Generals of all the Allies for beginning the War there, and the great Alacrity and Chearfulness with which they always sent their Troops to Fight under our General, is sufficient to License and approve the Measures enter'd into, for carrying on the War in *Flanders*, tho' a much less prosperous Event had attended our Arms. Or why, if it were a wrong step, did the most consumate Generals the World ever knew, go into it so readily, that all our Allies, all our Generals, and all the World shou'd be mistaken but the **Conducter** is very strange. That the *Emperor*, when even his own Territories were threatend with an Invasion, the dreadful Effects of which he had just before Experienc'd, shou'd send such a Body of Troops to *Flanders*, with the best General in the World at the Head of Them, to do nothing, or, at least, what was quite wrong, is another Mystery; and a greater Mystery than all, is, that no Body shou'd know this but the **Conducter** and his Friends.

Well, but however it was wrong begun, 'tis certainly (the Event having answer'd beyond our Expectation) the only Place now, (where by a little more patience, if the **Conducter** and his Friends were not in such haste for a scurvy Peace) to bring *France* to such Terms, as shou'd put it out of her Power, to begin a new War upon us, at the hazard of imposing the *Pretender* with it, in any little compass of Time: He is willing to allow that the Conditions of Peace, turn upon the Events of War, and yet seems very tender of having it press'd too strongly against the *French* King, as if he was sensibly concern'd to ward off any Blow on that side. From whence we may venture to draw this Supposition, that tho' such a Peace as he lays down, may be necessary for us to accept, will it do him

of

or us any harm, if we can at this time obtain a better? Was there any necessity to betray our selves for fear the Events of Peace, shou'd rise too high for us? Cou'd we not have Treated with the *French*, without making our Condition so wretched, and plainly, telling Them, that if They grant us any better Terms than we hint at, They are Unwise, since we have a Party ready to Embrace even Them, bad as They are, open Mouth'd: A Blessed Story, when it shall be told to our Children, Drench'd in Blood, and Involv'd in new Misfortunes, thro' our headlong Mistakes, and unhappy Oversights. What will the World say, but laugh at us and our Divisions; and when we shou'd hereafter want the Assistance of our Allies, to be able to obtain of them, not so much as their Pity.

But I return from this ungrateful Subject, to the *Flanders-War*: Since the Judgment of our Allies, and all our Generals, will not pass for Reason, with the Conducter and his Friends, there is no dispute to be made, but they will agree to the Sentiments of their own Friends. What is it the Enemy have more dreaded at any Time, than the Progress of our Arms in *Flanders*? And what Difficulties have they struggled under to oppose us there? And what drew them to make us submissive Offers of Peace, both after the *Ramellies*, and *Lille* Campagnes, but the Effect of our wondrous Successes in *Flanders*, and the Dread of our penetrating quite thro' a broken Frontier? And what is the meaning, that *Spain*, and the *Indies*, shou'd be offer'd us then, if we had been wise enough to take it; and now, after we have, by new unheard of Successes almost swallow'd up the Remainder of that Frontier, we are to bate of our Demands, and receive dishonourable Conditions from a beaten and dispirited Enemy? Is our Case so very hard and irretrievable, that we must never hope to have this fairly explain'd, till it is too late, and till our Enemies are in a Capacity of protecting those, who have so faithfully serv'd them.

Again, If *Flanders* were not the right Place to push the Enemy in, why are they so very apprehensive of our Efforts, that they seek and contrive all manner of ways to divert our Arms there? What Time is there to be nam'd, when in the Interval of any Campagne, they have not threatned with terrible Denuntiations to invade the Empire, or drive our Forces out of *Spain* the next Spring. Their *Letters*, their *Gazettes* have been full of it; and what was all this for, but to divert the Course of the War in *Flanders*? which they found pinch'd them so hard, and was likely to pinch harder, if nothing cou'd stop our Courier: Nay, what was the *Scotch* Expedition for, but for the same Reason, that they were willing to run all Hazards to divert the Current of the War in *Flanders*, but all this by the good Conduct of our M——rs and G——l was wonderfully defeated, and has set us as much above the necessity of accepting what the Enemy contemptibly offer, as we ought to prefer a glorious and successful War, to an ignominious and precarious Peace.

I think nothing more need be said to prove, that the Clamour rais'd against the *Method of carrying on the War*, is like all the other Arguments made use of by the **Conducter**, false and nefarious; only tinsel'd over with gay and glittering Words, to serve a present *Purpose*, without being sufficient to stand the Test of future Enquiry. Indeed I might have added, That the War in *Flanders*, lay so hard on the Enemy, as occasion'd the *French* King to draw his Forces out of *Spain*, to oppose us on that Side; and that it was the sole Reason of his offering to abandon his Grandson, and which he wou'd now be content with, were our Friends at Home, but half as civil as our Enemies Abroad.

The

The next Part of his Proposition is, *That we suffer'd all our Allies to break every Article of those Treaties and Agreements by which they were bound, and to lay all the burden upon us.* This bold Assertion is not to be wonder'd at, taking the rest along with it, for what can be said less, after the Treatment they have been expos'd to, which was no more than a necessary Conclusion, that we might now break all our Articles with them? To enter into the Proof of this, he first offers some *Remarks* on certain *Articles* in Three of our *Treaties, viz.* the *Barrier Treaty*, and our *Two Alliances* with *Portugal*, Offensive and Defensive; from whence it might reasonably be judged, that these were some of those *Treaties* that are pretended to be broke, whereas Two of them do no way come into the Dispute. The First, particularly, do's not concern the Operations of the War and therefore, in reality, has nothing to do here, unless, as necessary to serve a Purpose, that of railing at the *Dutch*, and ridiculing the late M—y, for endeavouring to establish a firm Union between the Two Nations, for the Advantage and Security of both. One wou'd think no Objection cou'd be made to this *Treaty*; nor, indeed, wou'd it ever have happen'd, but that, according to some present Schemes, we are oblig'd to take something from the *Dutch*, that we may be in a Capacity of complimenting the Enemy with the securest Part of their *Barrier*, in case of a Peace. But to fall in with his Objections against the Substance of this *Treaty*, he says, *First— That neither Her Majesty, nor Her Kingdoms, have any Interest or Concern in it, farther than what is mention'd in the Second, and Twentieth Articles: By the former of which the States are to assist the Queen in defending the Act of Succession; and, by the other, not to treat of Peace, till the King of* France *acknowledges the Queen, and the Succession of* Hannover, *and promises to remove the* Pretender *out of his Dominions.* Are not these now most surprizing and dangerous Objections? that we shou'd offer to concert with a

power-

powerful Neighbour and Ally, the Means of streng-thening our Act of Succession? And what greater Interest can the Qu— or Kingdom have, than such a *Treaty* gives them? What *Englishman* that has these Things at Heart, and dreads the Mischiefs of *Popery*, and *Arbitrary Power*, but must look on the **Coducter** with the utmost Indignation, while he sees him treating the Care of the *Protestant Succession* with so much contempt; especially when he considers with what Insolence the *French* King treats Her Majesty's Title in the late Offers of Peace, in such Words, as give a just occasion for Distrust. But what do's the **Conducter** mean? Can a Point, which so nearly concerns us, be too well secur'd? or, Is he afraid it shou'd be so? Whatever his Intentions be, the Sense of the Nation, in Parliament, has been otherwise; and he knows, very well, that the *Barrier Treaty* was transacted in pursuance of an Address of both Houses, and in execution of the Q—'s own Sense, ex-press'd in Her Answer to them. And will any body now pretend, that Points, recommended by P—t, and approv'd by the Crown, ought to be thus trea-ted, whatever the Reasons may be for recalling our own Act and Deed? But the **Conducter** is pleas'd to observe, *That it is certainly for the Interest and Safety of the States General, that the Protestant Succession shou'd be preserv'd in* England, and therefore infers, That 'tis unnecessary to bind them by any other Obligation. By the same Rule, he must acknowledge it is our Interest and Concern to preserve the *Low-Countries* from falling into the Hands of *France*, and that we can have no greater Security, than by insisting on a sufficient *Barrier* for the *Dutch*, the larger the better. And, is it not necessary, therefore, in concert, to take all the care we can to preserve those Two Points, mutually between each other, and may not Things that are necessary to be done be sometimes omitted. Do's he not charge our Allies with having neglected their Quota's, and yet it was plainly their

Interest

Intereſt not to do ſo? Now can it be a Subject of difference to ſtrengthen our Intereſt in Them, by a matter that wou'd coſt us ſo little, or allowing Them a Point which we cou'd loſe ſo little by? And in which our own Intereſt and Security is as much involv'd as Theirs? *What an Impreſſion*, ſays he, *of our Settlement muſt it give Abroad, to ſee our Miniſters offering ſuch Conditions to the* Dutch, *to prevail with Them to be Guarantees to our Acts of Parliaments.* What wou'd this Man make of this? Is our Calling in the *Dutch* to be Guarantees of our Succeſſion, which he ſays himſelf they are concern'd in, prevailing with him to be Guarantees to our Acts of Parliaments? Is it not the ſame Thing that we are Guarantees for their Barrier? which, indeed, there is no more occaſion for, than the other, but to ſhew the mutual Friendſhip that ought to Reign between us, for our mutual Security. Nor is the Right he ſpeaks on ſo well Eſtabliſh'd, but the aſſiſtance of the *Dutch* may hereafter become neceſſary to preſerve it, and equivalent to any Exorbitant Article in the Treaty he finds Fault with on Their ſide. But why theſe unneceſſary Cavils againſt the *Dutch* at this Time, 'tis plain They have a Right to their Barrier previous to this Treaty, as may be ſeen by the 5th Article of the Grand Alliance, which expreſly ſays, *That the Allies ſhall uſe Their utmoſt Endeavours to recover the* Spaniſh-Netherlands, *to the end they may ſerve as a Fence, Rampart and Barrier to keep* France *at a diſtance from the* United-Provinces, *as formerly; the* Spaniſh-Netherlands *having been the Security of the* States-General, *till the late ſeizure of Them by the* French *King.* Likewiſe in the 9th Article 'tis ſaid, *That the Allies at a Treaty of Peace, ſhall agree on what are the proper ways to ſecure the* States-General, *by the aforeſaid Barrier*, Purſuant to which Articles, as faſt as the Towns in *Flanders* have been taken, the *Dutch* have Garriſon'd them, by the unanimous conſent of the Allies; and 'tis for the

ſame

same Reason in the 22d, and 23d, Articles of the Preliminary Treaty agreed, *That as well the Towns which did not belong to the Crown of* Spain, *at the Death of King* Charles II. *as those that did, which* France, *by those Articles was to deliver up, shou'd be yielded and made over to the* States, *to serve for their Barrier, and to be Garrison'd by their Troops.* So that in the Barrier Treaty we may see, after all the Clamour about it, that Her Majesty in reality agrees, to no more than to support the States in a sufficient Barrier, such as had been granted Them before by all the Allies, and under such Regulations as were every way necessary to support it, without being in any manner inconsistent with the Honour and Interest of *Great-Britain.*

The 20th Article, he says, *is a natural consequence that must attend any Treaty of Peace, we can make with* France, *being only the Acknowledging of Her Majesty, as Queen of Her own Dominions, and the Right of Succession by Her own Laws, which no Foreign Prince has Power to dispute.* And is this all that the 20th Article is binding in? When he tells us himself but just before; *That no Peace shall be made with* France, *without a Promise to remove the Pretender out of his Dominions.* Nor does this Article barely insist on his Acknowledging Her Majesty, as Queen of Her own Dominions, or on the Right of Succession by our own Laws, which general Expressions, 'tis easy enough to elude, but on Her Majesties Title to the Crown of *Great-Britain,* and of the Right of Succession in the House of *Hanover,* as Establish'd by our Acts of Settlement; which is, by the said Articles, fully to be acknowledg'd by *France,* as a Preliminary, previous to any Treaty of Peace; and not left to be a Consequence of one, as he wittily pretends it must be. Nor was it found so at the Peace of *Reyswick,* since which time, the *French* King has denied the Q---s Title, and own'd the *Pretender,* and assisted him to Invade Her Dominions

minions. The next of his Objections is, against the Unreasonableness and Exorbitant Articles, which he says, are granted the States by the rest of the Treaty: And first---*That by the Grand Alliance the* Spanish Low-Countries *were to be recover'd, and deliver'd to the King of* Spain, *but by his Treaty, that Prince is to possess nothing in* Flanders, *during the War.* This is falsely represented again, for 'tis no where said by the *Grand-Alliance*, that the *Low-Countries* shou'd be deliver'd to the King of *Spain*, much less during the *War*: And, 'tis well known, that long before this *Treaty* was made, the Government of those conquer'd Places has been administred by the *Queen*, and the *States*, with the consent of the *Emperor*, and King *Charles*, and were never design'd, as I think appears plain enough, to be deliver'd up to King *Charles*, tho' this *Treaty* had never been transacted: But yet, to shew the regard that was had to that Prince's Interest, it is expresly reserv'd, that the Sovereignty of those *Provinces*, both as to their Civil and Ecclesiastical Rights, shall be and remain to him, as well in those Towns where the *Dutch* are to have Garrisons, as where they are to have none; that of the Military Command being only reserv'd for the *Dutch*, in the Towns which they are allow'd to Garrison: These the Conducter makes to be about 20 in number, with their Dependencies; for which, he says, *The* Dutch, *after a Peace, are to have* 400000 *Crowns a Year from the King of* Spain, *to maintain their Garrisons; by which means they will have the command of all* Flanders, *from* Newport *to* Namur, *and be entirely Masters of the* Pais de Wais, *the richest Part of those Provinces.* Now he shou'd have distinguish'd between those Towns in this *Barrier*, which were in the possession of the Crown of *Spain*, at the death of K. *Charles* II. and those that were not, for of the last only, and their Dependencies, the *Dutch* are to have the Revenues, with the addition of 400000 Crowns yearly, for maintaining the whole

Barrier;

Barrier; which, considering the great number of Troops that it will require, and the vast Expence of keeping up and repairing the Fortifications, and supplying those Places with all warlike Necessaries, and the ruin'd condition they find the Country in, it must be allow'd, the *Dutch* have no such Bargain of it, and that nothing but their own Preservation cou'd have prevail'd with them to have engag'd themselves in such a hazardous and troublesome Undertaking.

He farther adds, *That the* Dutch *have liberty to Garrison any Places, in the* Low-Countries, *they think fit, whenever there is an appearance of a War, and, consequently, to put Garrisons in* Ostend, *or where else they please, upon a Rupture with* England. This unlucky Hint of a *Rupture* with *England*, the **Conducter** seems very fond of, tho' 'tis all a very frivolous Assertion: For, *First*, the *Dutch* have no right to this liberty, of putting Garrisons into such Places as they please, but in case, where they are attack'd, or in apparent danger, which is chiefly with a view to *France*, against whose Insults, Experience shews they can never be too securely on their Guard And it may be possible, by the Intrigues of *France*, that *Others* may join with Her against them, as they have done in former *Wars*, and may do again, from whom, 'tis very reasonable, that They ought to be guarded. But as to a *Rupture* with Us, 'tis out of the Question, and what, I hope, will never happen; And shou'd the Friends of *France* prevail in that Point, I think we shou'd scarce go to *Flanders* to attack them. Nay, in case we did, this Article can never hurt us, unless we break with the *Emperor* at the same Time, because 'tis otherwise impossible for the *Dutch* to put Troops into *Ostend*, since, by this very *Treaty*, that Place is entirely left in the Hands of the *Emperor*, and to be Garrison'd by him.

His next Objection is, *That the* Dutch, *by this Treaty, will be, in effect, Masters of all the* Low-Countries; *may impose Duties, Restrictions in Commerce, and Prohibitions, at their pleasure; and in the fertile Country, may set up all sorts of Manufactures particularly Woollen, by inviting the disoblig'd*

Manufacturers in Ireland, *and the* French Refugees, *who are scatter'd all over* Germany. What an accumulated Heap of false Assertions is here? merely contriv'd on purpose to terrifie and incense the People of *England* against this *Treaty*, without having the least ground of Truth in it. I think nothing is plainer than what I have prov'd already, That the Civil Power, with all the Rights and Privileges belonging to it, is expresly to remain in the *Emperor*, how then can it be said, that the *Dutch*, who have only the Military Power, shou'd impose Duties, Restrictions, *&c.*? But, suppose it at worst, even as he represents, yet it is very far from being liable to such dreadful Consequences as he sets forth. The principal trading Towns, as *Amsterdam, Harlem, Leyden,* and the rest, will make it their care to prevent the establishing new Manufacturers in that Country, which they wou'd never hitherto suffer, even in those ancient Places, that have appertain'd to the States, from the Time of the *Munster-Treaty*: So that shou'd the disoblig'd Manufacturers of *Ireland* attempt to settle in any of the Towns compriz'd in this Treaty, it is very probable they will find themselves worse treated than they were in their own Country. Another frightful Objection against this Treaty, is, *That all the Ports in* Flanders *are to be subject to the like Duties the* Dutch *shall lay upon the* Scheld, *which is to be clos'd on the Side of the States. Thus all other Nations are in effect shut out from trading with* Flanders; yet, in the very same Article, 'tis said, *That the States shall be favour'd in all the* Spanish *Dominions, as much as* Great Britain, *or as the People most favour'd.* This now has no more in it, after all the colour given to it, to make us look like an injur'd People, but that all Matters relating to Commerce, shall be put upon the same Foot, as they were in before the War, when it was always thought we had as much Right and Favour as the *Dutch*: Besides, is it not a frivolous, as well as false Assertion, *That other Nations are, in effect, shut out from trading with* Flanders, when I have so plainly shew'd before, that all the

Civil

Civil Right is lodg'd in the *Emperor*, of which there never cou'd have been any danger, but from the unreasonable Provocation that has been given to our Allies, by the Friends of *France*: Besides, for avoiding all difference between the Two Nations on this Head, in pursuance of the *Grand-Alliance*; the Q—— and the States do not only by this Article mutually engage to preserve Commerce upon the same Foot it was before the War, but engage that the Subjects of each shall be treated alike, and as favourable as those of any other Nation, in all Parts of the *Spanish Dominions*. Therefore to say that we are in danger as to our Trade, by this *Barrier Treaty*, is utterly false; or we have conquer'd *Flanders* for our selves, as well as the *Dutch*, and by this *Treaty* our own Trade is re-establish'd and secur'd as well as theirs. What then the design of all this violent Resentment can be, against a Treaty so very reasonable in it self, and even advantagious to our selves, is very unaccountable, and it will be out of the power of any One to imagine, unless from the scandalous Intimation the Conducter has given us; *That it has put it out of the power of our own Legislature to change our Succession without the consent of our Guarantee*. Which, I think, take it under what Construction you please, ought to add a double value to so beneficial an Alliance.

I think it is Time to have done with this Head. Let us next examine into our Alliances with *Portugal*, which, because they stand equally in the way of an unsafe Peace, are under the same necessity of being damn'd with the *Barrier-Treaty*. In speaking of these *Treaties*, in order the more clearly to justifie the transacting them, the Reader ought to be pre-advis'd to consider what Circumstances Affairs stood in at that Time, and the great Influence the *French* have in that Court, as all who are competent Judges in the matter, do very well know, and then it cannot but be look'd upon as the Effect of the most refin'd Politicks, that they were to be drawn off from their Engagements at all; which, in respect to the good State of our Enemies Affairs at that Time, had been impossible to do, had not the most ardent Courage and Resolution of the King of *Portugal*, contributed beyond any Thing that humane Prudence cou'd have devis'd. Now in consideration of so great a Benefit to the common Cause, as was reasonably expected from these Alliances, let us see how much we over-reach'd them, by the Terms granted in the Treaty.

Both the Offensive and Defensive Alliance were made at the same Time, and sign'd the same Day, *viz.* 16 *May*, 1703. The First consists of XXIX Articles, in which 'tis agreed, *That for the Land-Service, and the Invasion of* Spain *on that Side, the King of* Portugal, *shall maintain, at his own Expence,* 15000 *Men, and raise* 13000 *more to be paid by the Allies.* And to this Body of *Portugueze-Troops*, the Allies are to join 12000 *Men of their own, or other Nations.* This is the Substance of the First 16 Articles; the Two next, which are those that the Conducter is so angry at, relate chiefly to the Sea-Service. By the First, the Maritime Powers are oblig'd, *to keep on the Coast of* Portugal, *a competent number of Men of War to defend their Ports, and protect their Trade.* Then follows, That upon certain Advice, that the Enemy intend to invade them with a superior Force to what the Allies shall have on their Coast, that they shall increase their number of Ships, so as to be able to protect them; and that such Ships shall continue in those Seas, or Ports, so long as His *Portugueze* Majesty shall judge necessary. In the next Article, they, (the Allies) oblige themselves, for the defence of the *Portugueze* Dominions beyond Seas; And we lately see how well we kept this Article of our Treaty, where, I do not find, that we had one Ship, either to protect them, or our selves: And this upon certain Advice, that they are design'd to be invaded, in which Case, if any strong Place be taken from them, we are to continue our Assistance till it is re-taken. What is there now in these Articles so unreasonable for the *Portugueze* to ask, or we to grant? Was it reasonable that His *Portugueze* Majesty shou'd break with *France*, to support our Interest, and expose

himself

himself to the Insults and Invasions of such powerful Enemies by Sea and Land, which he knew himself in no condition to withstand, and not so much as demand to be protected from the Naval Strength of *France*, which cou'd not be done, but by keeping a Squadron upon his Coast, and increasing it upon any sudden Notice of an Invasion; and this He impertinently calls, *taking the King of* Portugal'*s Word, whenever he has a Fancy he shall be invaded, or when he is in a Humour to apprehend an Invasion.* Is not this imposing, in the grossest manner, upon the Judgment of all those concern'd in the Treaty, as well as those who read, such intollerable Reasoning? Do not the very Words of the Treaty say, *upon certain Knowledge or Advice?* And who is the most proper Person for this Knowledge to come from, but the King himself? Ought not Princes to be allow'd to have the quickest and best Intelligence of their own danger? And are our Admirals such Novices, that they are to be govern'd by Humour and Fancy, and not be suffer'd to have the Conduct to know when they are impos'd on? And if they find, or conceive they are so, may they not, by their own Instructions, refuse to go upon such Errands? But there is this Fate in its lying expos'd to the Conducter's Insults, that I do not think it possible to express so advantagious an Alliance in any better, or, indeed, in any other manner, considering, that in all Treaties, something is, of course, to be left to the Faith and Honour of the Prince, or State, it is concluded with; and how easily they are eluded, and broke into, when any Caprice serves turn, he has himself given us a very glaring Instance of.

Another Thing offends the Conducter, and that is, *That these Fleets must not only be subject to the King, but to his Vice Roys, Admirals, and Governors, which,* he says, *is an Indignity that was never offer'd before, except in a conquer'd Nation.* How vile an Inference is this? The Substance of which is express'd thus, *That all auxiliary Ships shall be subject to the King's Orders; and in Parts beyond the Seas, to the Orders of His Vice-Roys and Governors.*

This is no more than saying, That they shall be apply'd to the use they were agreed on. For I wou'd ask the Conducter, If all Auxiliaries are not subject to the supreme Command, in whatever Place they serve in? And this is no more than necessary, to avoid all *Disputes* and *Disorders* that might otherwise arise, and render their Service useless: And, again, whatever is necessary to make an Alliance useful, can never be said, with Reason, to be an Indignity. So that whatever he has urg'd against these 4 Articles, is both malicious and absurd; since nothing has been agreed on, which was less than *Portugal* cou'd ask, or we cou'd grant, without derogating from the Honour of our Country.

In the Defensive Alliance, which is perpetual, the Articles, relating to our Shipping, are much the same, and therefore are to be answer'd by the same Words, but the Conducter do's not care to meddle with the 8th Article, which has this difference, *That if the Ships of any of the Three Nations are to act in conjunction, in any Expedition which is the common Concern of them all,* (and not in particular to *Portugal*) *that then the Commander, who has most Ships under him, shall give the Signal, and act in all respects, as Admiral of the whole.* 'Twas by this Article that Sir *John Leake*, in 1705, had under him a Flag of *Portugal*, with the Flower of the Navy-Royal. His Quarrels, at this Treaty, are, in many Points, so very frivolous, that it is no easie matter to pick out any Thing that deserves an Answer, of this Species is the Assertion following, *That if* We *or* Holland *are invaded, yet if we expect any Assistance from the King of* Portugal, *we are to supply him with Forces in the same manner as if he were invaded himself, which,* he infers, *must needs be a very prudent course for a Maritime Power to take, upon a sudden Invasion, by which, instead of making use of our Fleets and Armies for our own defence, we must send them abroad for the defence of* Portugal. Now, is it possible to expect, when there is such a vast disproportion in the Strength of the Parties who are to manage this Alliance, that the Assistance on each Side shou'd be equal, wou'd it not be an unreasonable Thing, to ask One of the petty Electors to furnish as much toward the War, as the Emperor Himself? It is the same Thing here, when the publick Service shall render a Diversion on the Side of *Portugal* of advantage, wou'd it be any Crime to make such an addition to their native Strength, as might, in all probability, enable them to do it to purpose, which their own Force was not sufficient for? And if otherwise we think it more for our service to keep our Ships and Men at Home, do these Articles substitute us to the contrary, but upon our own voluntary choice? But the Conducter seems to mean, that he wou'd have the K. of *Portugal* make some extraordinary Effort of himself, to assist us, in case we are invaded; and, in truth, so wou'd I too, but that I, and all Mankind know it is not in his power, and this is, indeed, the true Reason why the *Dutch* have not continu'd to perform their part in the First of these Alliances: For, as to the Second, as I have shewn, it do's not properly take place yet: And, if we have kept closer to our Articles than the *Dutch*, it was, and is, because they are of much more consequence to us, in respect to the real Benefits we reap from thence in our Trade.

They who remember how impatient the Nation were to have these Alliances made, before they were enter'd into, and what hopes we had of reducing *Spain*, by an Impression on that side, on which the whole Country lies open to *Madrid*, as has been experienced by one or two happy Events, tho' not prudently or successfully follow'd: And the inevitable Ruin and Decay, not only of our Spanish Trade, but that of the *Mediterranean* also, which must certainly have follow'd, if the Port of *Lisbon* had continu'd shut to us: All, I say, who remember this, must allow, That instead of blaming the late M——y, there are no Thanks or Praises too much for them And had our Expectations answer'd in all respects, from those Treaties, as well in the Advantages of War as Trade, which, by the way, no body cou'd foresee they wou'd not, they wou'd have been worth to us infinitely more than what, by the Terms of the Treaty, we were to have given the *Portugueze* in lieu of them: Nor do I believe, if the War were to continue, even the new M——y wou'd advise the breaking of them; while it is plain that the Advantages of our Trade, sufficiently overballance all the Inconveniencies we are said to receive from them, nor has it happen'd from the Articles themselves, but from the ill Execution of some of them, which was almost unavoidable. The Treaty made with that Prince at the end of the Year 1703, for admitting our English Cloth, which at that time stood Prohibited in *Portugal*, is, of it self, of more real Advantage to us, than any thing they cou'd reap by us. Their own Manufactures were immediately ruin'd by it; and both *Portugal*, and its Dominions in *America*, have ever since been forced to depend on us for their *Wollen Goods*: Besides, we have in a manner carried on the Spanish Trade thro' them, and almost engrost the whole return of Bullion from *Brazil*, which behov'd us to have taken a little more care of that Trade than it appears we have done. Nor this only, but our Troops in *Spain* and *Portugal* have been chiefly pay'd by the Advantages of the Balances of Trade on that side, without sending any Species from *England*. This the Conducter very well knows; but these Ends are not compriz'd within the Reasons of his exclaiming against these Alliances, which are the same in the main, with his wrangling so heartily at the *Barrier-Treaty*, *viz*. Because the latter secures to the *Dutch* such Towns, as by such a Peace as he writes for, are to be given back to *France*, which cannot be done till we have taken them from our Allies for that purpose; and by our Alliances with *Portugal*, we are engag'd not to leave the Duke of *Anjou* in possession of *Spain* and the *Indies*. We may remember how oft it has been said, the *French* would endeavour to divide the Allies; and what Application these things afford, the World is to judge.

After all this clamour against the substance of our

Treaties, which I have shewn, were no otherwise faulty, than as they stood in the way of such a Peace as the **Conducter** is writing for, he comes at length to prove, as he calls it, *That we suffer'd each of our Allies to break every Article in their Treaties*, and in order to prove it, which is pleasant enough, he proposes negatively, *To consider in what manner they have observ'd those Treaties, &c.* And even this Charge is only against the Emperor, the *Dutch*, and the King of *Portugal*; and first the *Dutch*, whom he attacks in the manner following.

That whereas, by a Convention subsequent to the Grand Alliance, 'twas agreed, That Holland *shou'd bring into the Field* 60000 *Men in* Flanders; *and* England 40000, *yet there was an Augmentation made by the* Dutch *and us of* 20000 *Men, for the Year* 1703, *upon a Par directly contrary to the former Stipulation.* A very pretty way of proving that our Allies have broke their Treaties, by maintaining what indeed has nothing to do with them. That such an Augmentation was made, and upon a Par, we all know, but how it is contrary to any former Stipulation is a Mystery, because it was built upon an Agreement perfectly new, and upon new Conditions; and chiefly, that if we agreed to this Argumentation upon a Par, it was insisted by our P——t, at that time the *Dutch* shou'd prohibit their Commerce with *France*, which with the benefit of the Augmentation, they thought was a hard Bargain enough; however, for the good of the Common Cause, they consented to it for one Year, but finding by Experience, that their People neither cou'd nor wou'd bear with it any longer. Our P——t was contented to continue the Augmentation, without obliging the *Dutch* to this hardship. Besides, this Augmentation upon a Par, was not breaking any former Stipulation, but making a new one, and if any new Regulations are to be made, are not the *Dutch* at liberty as well as we, to make the best Terms they can for themselves. It wou'd be, in effect, arguing, That in any War that shall break out for the future, we shall oblige the States of *Holland* to an observance,

servance of all the Articles now in force, either for or against them. This is the true State of the first Augmentation that was made, and we might have refus'd it if we wou'd. It is certain the *Dutch* made the greatest Effort imaginable, at their first setting out, and rais'd above 60000 Men, besides 45000 they had in their pay before the War began, which was so heavy a charge, that they soon found they cou'd not bear the Expence of taking any more Troops into their Service, jointly with *England* upon the first Foot.

His next Charge is *That the next, and some ensuing Campagnes farther additional Forces were allow'd, and in every new Supply the* Dutch *gradually lessen'd their Proportions.* But to satisfie the Reader in the Falsity of this, we shall here shew what Forces the *Dutch* Annually contracted, after the aforesaid Augmentation of 10000 Men in 1703.

The next Year 1704, the States took into their Service one Regiment of Dragoons, and three of Foot of *Wirtembergh*, making 4000 Men.	4000
In the Year 1706, they took together with *Great-Britain*, by Contract, two Regiments of Horse, and a Batallion of *Hessians*, by which their Body of 9000 Men was augmented, the States share is 600.	600
And by a 2d Contract the same Month together with *Great Britain*, 3000 *Palatines*; the States 3d Part is 1000.	1000
In the beginning of the Year 1707, the States augmented their National Horse with 8 Men in each Company, amounting to 1160.	1160
By a Contract of *April* 30. the same Year, *Great Britain* and the *States* took into their service 4639 *Palat.* their share.	2319
Again, by Contract the 27th of *August*, the same Year, 1 Regiment of Dragoons of 800 Men, the States, half 400.	400
The States besides, took into their Service by a Contract of the 21st of *February* 1707, two Regiments of Foot of *Wolfembuttel* making 1400 Men.	1400
By another Contract, *March* 22. the same Year, together with *Great-Britain*, 4092 *Saxons*, the *States* Share,	2046
Likewise by that of the same Month, One Regiment of Foot, of *Hostein Gottorp*, of 797.	797
And by another Contract, 18 *April*, 1 of *Munster* of 800 Men.	800
The *States* did at the same time augment the *Swiss* and *Grison* Regiments, with 22 Men in each Company making 1144 Men.	1144

And,

And, Lastly, the *States* agreed, the 20th of *June*, 1711 for a *Swiss* Regiment of 1200 Men, which is now raising, and in good Forwardness 1200

Now, where is this lessening their Proportions, gradually every Year, from the Augmentation that was made in 1703, at a Par? Besides which, 'tis observeable, that all the Troops, set down in this Account, on their Part of the Supplies, receive of ordinary Pay of the States, and Money of them more, One *Hessian* Regiment excepted; whereas *Great-Britain* has allow'd theirs, besides One Regiment of the *Langraves*, a Body of *Hanoverians*, and 6000 *Prussians*, a much Lower Pay, so that they only supply their Wants by means of the Winter-Quarters they have in the Flat Countries. And, 'tis likewise to be observ'd, that, besides the Troops beforemention'd, the States pay since the Year 1706, together with Her Britanick Majesty; the Bread Forage, and Agio of the Money at 26 *per Cent.* for a Body of 10370 *Prussians*; and that this Payment, do's in Relation, come so much the nearer to the ordinary Pay, because a great Part of that Body has every Year it's Winter Quarters in the Flat Countries of of the State, which prevents geting in the Taxes, which otherwise wou'd turn to Account; so that there is good Reason to infer that the States pay One Half of that Body, which is 5185 Men.

By all this, the Reader may see that the States have not only born their due Proportion from the first Augmentation, but have made several Additions to the Troops in their Service, in which we bore no Share at all; so that nothing can be more false than to say, *That in every new Supply the* Dutch *gradually lessen'd their Proportions.* Whereas; the First Augmentation was made upon a Par, and, at least, it must be granted, that so were all that have been made since, for the service of *Flanders*. There were indeed in the Year 1706, 3000 *Palatines* taken into the Service of Us and the States, of which we pay two Thirds, but then these Troops, tho' put on the *Flanders* Establishment,

ment, never served there but in *Spain*, the Service at that time requiring it: And besides, in lieu of this, the States increased their Horse against next Year with 8 Men in a Troop, amounting in the whole to 1200 Men, which is more than their Proportion, according to the first Augmentation at a Par. And as to the Parliamentary Addresses to the Q——n, *That the States might be desir'd to observe their Proportions*; the Reader is to kvow that whatever was done of this kind, was upou general Rumours only, and not upon any Facts that appeared before the House; nor is there any thing more groundless, than the Effect he pretends these Addresses had upon the States. *That they eluded them by making their Troops* Nominal Corps, *which they did by keeping up the Number of Regiments, and sinking a 5th Part of the Men and Money*. Whereas in Truth, the *Dutch* Corps are so far from being Nominal, that they are esteem'd to be the compleatest in the whole Service, no Troops are so strictly muster'd, once, at least, every Campaign, and every Captain is oblig'd upon pain of being Cashier'd, to have his Complment to a Man.

The next Complaint is the most frivolous thing that I think can be said by any Man that pretends to be in his Senses. *The more Towns*, says he, *we Conquer, the worse condition we are in, because they make no scruple of employing the Troops of their Quota, towards Garrisoning every Town, as fast as it is taken, directly contrary to the Agreement, by which Garrisons are excluded*. This is so empty a Notion, that all who know any thing of the matter, must allow that Frontier Garrisons are the strength of an Army, else it might properly be said, That the Enemy are stronger, and in a better Condition for every Town that is taken from them, because we are the weaker for every Man we put into Garrison; which wou'd be a pretty way of arguing. But to leave this to those who are better Soldiers than either the Conducter or my self; what he alledges is otherwise no more than a mere Equivocation; for if he wou'd give us the Words of this A-

greement,

greement, we shou'd find; *That the Garrisons excluded,* mean no more than the Garrisons of the Towns, which at that time belonged to the States, and not those that shou'd be taken from the Enemy, in the Prosecution of the War. Besides, it is known to those who understand such *Affairs*, that what *Troops* remains in Garrison, are but a Trifle in comparison of the whole Army, and generally of such Regiments as suffer'd most the Campaign before, and scarce in a Condition to take the Field. As to those Towns which lie nearest to the Enemy, they have indeed larger Garrisons, but, at the same time, as I have observ'd, they are as useful for the Service of the War as those in the Field: First, in regard for securing our Convoys, and other extraordinary Services; and likewise, That upon any Emergency, the greatest part of them may join the Army upon the least Signal. Now if the Conducter be so good a Proficient in the Art of War, to tell us which way we shall find Troops to put into the Towns we take, without drawing them from the Army, I shall believe the *Dutch*, by pursuing such a Method, have broke their Alliance.

This at length, he asserts, arriv'd to such a heighth, *That there are at present in the Field, not so many Forces under the D. of* M——— *s command in* Flanders, *as* Britain *alone maintains for that Service, nor have been for some Years past.* One would have thought it out of the Power of Malice to have suggested any thing so foolish and absurd! That if there was nothing else in his whole Book, this alone were, in a reasonable Community, enough to destroy the Credit of all he has said. In the Estimate of the Troops in Her Majesty's pay in *Flanders*, it appears that they make something above 62000 Men, which may be computed at 52 Battalions of Foot, and 68 Squadrons of Horse; Now if the D. of *M.* has, for some Years past, beaten, push'd, and harrass'd the *French* Army, besides taking their Towns, with an Army consisting of no more than 52 Battalions, and 68 Squadrons when the Enemy were, at least, by their own Accounts, 170, or

180

180 Battalions, and above 200 Squadrons, it must certainly be allow'd, we are the more oblig'd to His Grace's Conduct, to do all this for us; which Acknowledgment, I find, the **Conducter** was unadvisedly drawn into, contrary to his constant and natural Reflections on that General, in other Parts of his *Libel*; but, 'tis to be presum'd, that his Reasons for blacking the *Dutch*, in this remarkable Instance, made him quite forget himself, or, by a wilful Mistake, to chuse the greatest instead of the least of Two Evils: Tho', at the same Time, it was an Error in a purpose, perhaps less significant; the blackest Arts being then on foot, to ruin and displace the D——, and render him contemptible in the Eyes of the People, which, it has since appear'd, is not possible to be done, neither by any Thing the **Conducter** can write, or his *Friends* devise for him.

But to pursue his Complaints against the *Dutch*, the next is, for their not complying with the D. of M—'s Project for Winter-Quarters last Year. And here I cannot but observe, to the Honour of the *States*, That neither in this, nor in any one Instance thro' his whole Book, do's he prove them to have broke any one *Treaty*. I do not find, by any Agreement, that they are oblig'd to come into all the Projects we propose; and if they did not come into this, it was not for the Reasons the **Conducter** lays down: That it was because the *Dutch* wou'd not lose, *the paultry Benefit arising by Contribution*: On the contrary, it is certain, that the *States* gave several prudent Reasons against this Project, alledging, That to croud such a number of Troops upon the Frontier, wou'd, in many respects, be very inconvenient, and not only render them unfit for service at the opening of the Campagne, but leave the *Netherlands*, and their own *Provinces*, too much expos'd; and that the extraordinary Expence for Building, Stabling and other necessary Charges, was too great for them to bear, considering the prodigious Expence they were already at. However, for the good of the common Cause, provided the Troops

of

of the ſeveral Nations, in that Service, wou'd furniſh their *Quota* toward theſe Cantonments, and the Q— wou'd come into a proportion of the other Articles, beſides Forrage, they wou'd agree to it. This Project the E. of *St—rs* came over with ſo early as *July* laſt. But ſo long Time was taken here before it was conſented to, that it was forc'd to be laid aſide, tho' the beſt care had been taken, that the Execution of it might not be loſt for want of Time.

As to *the paultry benefit of Contributions*, the *Dutch* have ſufficiently clear'd themſelves in that Point, by ſhewing, That the *Treaty* for *Contributions* was made before this Deſign was form'd, and interfer'd but little therewith, *viz.* to hinder the Enemy from erecting Magazines ſince the ſaid *Treaty* for *Contributions* only ſays, *That the Product of thoſe Countries, under Contribution, ſhall paſs free and unmoleſted.* But the Product of that Country was entirely eaten up by our Armies, and therefore the *French-Magazines* muſt be made of what is not the Product of that Country, and, conſequently, are not affected by this *Treaty*. By which, it appears, that the Conducter's *paultry Benefit* had no part in it: Tho', at other Times, 'tis a *Benefit* which he will not allow to be a *paultry* one, when he, and his Friends, endeavour to make it amount to a mighty Sum, and to perſuade the World, that the D. of *M*— had a conſiderable Snack of it; tho', by this *Treaty*, they well know, that 'tis allotted to the *States*, in conſideration of the *Contributions* they pay themſelves, and of the vaſt Expence they are at in Sieges, which, by the ſucceſs of the War, and the loſs of Engineers, exceeds whatever cou'd have been expected or imagin'd they were able to bear. And, after all, if it were true, that the *States* did not agree to this *Propoſal*, to exert themſelves, who can blame them? With what Heart cou'd they enter into an expenſive Project for the War, when they were aſſur'd, that Negotiations for Peace were privately carry'd on, was it likely for them to expect a Project of ſuch importance, wholly form'd by the Duke of *M.* and highly for his Honour, wou'd be ſup-

ported,

ported, when Measures were then actually taken to supplant him, and where he had no longer any credit.

Again, I must observe, that, after all, this Project did not miscarry under the late M......y, which was a Point that the *Conducter* shou'd have prov'd, when he says, *That* WE *suffer'd our Allies to break all their Treaties.* Who he means by *WE*, I suppose, will be no otherwise interpreted, than to the *Old M....y*, when, if it had any ill Consequence, it was under the Influence of his *New Friends*. But, I believe, I may shew that it had no ill Consequence at all; for the *States*, so far comply'd with the Extent of it, as enabled us to prevent the Enemy from making any new Lines, which they intended, and cutting off *Bouchain*, as we may remember they afterwards attempted. And, for the rest of it, we see, in Fact, that they have since overturn'd all Objections to their Conduct at that Time, by burning the Enemies Magazines, the Foundation on which the Cavil was first built, which, perhaps, was then their Design, and has cost us much less than the cantoning such a vast number of Troops all Winter.

He now brings the *Dutch* to Account for their Navy-Affairs, and begins with saying, *That instead of making up their Fleet, what they fell short in their Army, they never once furnish'd their Quota either of Ships or Men.* I know some who bore considerable Commands in our Navy at that Time, and never made the least dispute of that then, till they were put on it to serve a *Purpose*, in being vexatious to our Allies. But, as I have already shewn, that they never did fall short in their Quota for the Army, but rather exceeded it, as appears by the List of their Forces, whereby they stand charg'd with the payment of 143385 Men, there was no Obligation to make any addition to their Fleet on that account. So I am likewise pretty well assur'd, that what they are charg'd withal, in relation to their Navy, will appear only some prudent Steps of good Husbandry and Frugality, and not any Contempt of Us, or Neglect of the Common-Cause, which they have zealously and constantly shewn to have so much at Heart: And this the *Conducter* seems to intimate himself. *Or if*, says he, *some few of their Ships, now and then, appear'd, it was no more than appearing, for they immediately separated, to look to their Merchants, and protect their Trade.* Which is a Thing they are, it seems, very careful in, and 'tis much for their Honour, as well as Advantage, they are so, which only can enable them, who are so small a State, to hold out so expensive a War, equivalent to their Neighbours, who have much larger Territories. And if this be retorted as a Reproach to them, I wish it cou'd be laid at our Door; who may remember, 'tis not much above a Twelve-month, since our *Virginia Fleet* was lost, upon our own Coast, for want of a little *Dutch-Care*.

But

But to judge of this more exactly, let us remember what it was we propos'd to do with our Fleets when the Proportions were settled at the beginning of the War; Was it not chiefly that we might be able to act offensively against the Common Enemy, as well by Sea as Land? And did not the States join heartily in this till we had gain'd our Point? Have the *French* ever been able to shew their Heads since the Fight at *Malaga*, 1704? Where we ought to remember how Serviceable the *Dutch Line* was, and what Encomiums both the Enemy and our selves bestow'd on 'em. And if they contributed their share till the point was gain'd, and the Enemy had no more a Fleet to put to Sea, ought they not to enjoy the benefit of doing double Service whilst they were at it? It is but natural to imagine that when the Quota's were first setled, it was upon a plain Supposition, that the Enemy would have such a Number of Ships at Sea, of which some near Computation might easily be made, and no doubt but it was made at that time. But we cannot concieve, nor imagine, that, if it cou'd have been suppos'd the Enemy wou'd not have kept out a Fleet, the Proportions on either side wou'd have been so large. And this I cannot but take to be a good Reason for their Frugality to save what might be sav'd: Or let me ask the Conductor, What they shou'd have done more with the Ships they sent to Sea? Since it appears on any Emergency, we had sufficient to execute our purpose. I can tell him, the *Dutch* are too Wise a People to be fond of Expeditions, and I believe, had they never such a number of Ships to spare, they wou'd send none to make Conquests in the *Indies*, or the Lord knows where; where, at best, they are liable to so many Accidents, as seldom fails to Ruin both the Ships and Troops employ'd on such Adventures; and this I think may be witness'd by our late Voyage to *Canada*, where it had been happy for us, had we, like our cautious Neighbours the *Dutch*, kept our Ships in our Harbours, or employ'd them in securing our

Trade; and not have suffer'd the Enemy to Sail after us with an Equivalent Squadron, and come Home at the Heels of us, big with the Plunder of our Faithful Allies; not wholly forgetting our Selves too.

He has still another Charge against the *Dutch*, *That these Guarrantees of our Succession, having not one Ship in the Mediterranean for many Months, they sent that part of their Quota thither, and furnish'd nothing to us, at the same time that they allarm'd us with the Rumour of an Invasion*. This is said to insult the *Dutch* as Guarrantees, by the Barrier Treaty, of our Succession; That being the hinge upon which all his Arguments turn. Now the Fact is this, It having been agreed, upon the consideration of the Posture of Affairs in *Spain* at that time, that the *English* and *Dutch* Squadrons shou'd Winter in the Mediterranean, contrary to what had been done in former Years, the States sent Two Expresses by Land to *Genoa*, and, as I remember, one by Sea; but all these unfortunately Missing their Admiral, he inadvertently return'd: Whereupon they immediatly fitted out another Squadron, which they lost no time in sending away. But now he talks of *the Rumour of an Invasion*; I remember indeed, about that time, we had such an Alarm; and that it gave great Offence, where is ought rather to have been Cherish'd: And because an Invasion did not actually follow, 'twas presently said to be a Plot of the *Dutch* and the late M——y, but I rather wish we don't Suffer another time for discouraging such useful Intelligence. And if no Invasion was so much as intended, I can't see where the Design of the *Dutch* cou'd be, upon a Supposition only to give us Notice: The *French* were at that time fitting out a Fleet, and making Preparations for an Invasion somewhere, tho' it fell in another Place; and the Pretender was sent on a sleeveless Errand to visit the Provinces of *France*, with no other purpose to be sure but to amuse us, and give occasion of a *Rumour of an Invasion*; and if the *Dutch* were too hasty in taking the Alarm, I believe there

there were Thousands in *England* of the same Mind, that were far from any Plot or Design against the Government. *But the Dutch sent their Ships to the Mediterranean, and furnish'd nothing to us:* There is the Complaint. Now I wou'd ask the **Conducter**, What occasion there was, if, as he says, 'twas only *the Rumour of an Invasion?* And whither they might not, notwithstanding the Squadron sent to the Mediterranean, have spar'd us on an Exigency Eight or Ten Men of War? The few Ships they sent upon that Service, were not all they were Masters of; or if indeed they were, I never heard that any Application was made to them to desire them to delay a while the Sailing of that Squadron, till the Rumour was over; And wou'd it not have been time enough to have given Assistance, when either our own Request, or the reality of the Danger had made it necessary.

In short, his Complaints against the *Dutch* are so many and so violent, that I grow even weary of taking notice of them; nor wou'd I indeed say more, but that the following is something remarkable; Sir *James Wishart*, he affirms, *met last Year with such a Reception, as ill became a Republick that lies under so many Obligations to us: In short, such a one, as those only deserve, who are content to take.* It happens here that the **Conducter** has blab'd out his Resentments from the real Sentiments of his Heart; he seems to think we shou'd demand Satisfaction; which he backs in another part of his Libel, where he says, *And we our selves may be under a necessity of recovering Towns out of the very Hands of those, for whom we are now Ruining our Country to take them,* I think these two Quotations, drawn into one entire Paragraph, give a plain intimation of the **Conducter**'s Good-will to the *Dutch*, and how reasonable he, and his Friends, (for I must always include them) wou'd at any time think another *Dutch War.* Their assisting us against King *James*, and being the original Spring of the Revolution, will not be forgiven them by some People, in ceeding Ages to come. But to the matter. As to the Reception of Sir *James Wishart*, he gives us no particulars how, or in what manner this Complaint is grounded, and therefore little is to be said to it at present: But I shall here observe in Justification of the States, that it is the first Complaint of this nature that has happen'd in Ten Years; and besides, that the *Dutch* did not comply in the Measures urg'd by Sir *James*, it was because they were neither able to do what was desired of them, nor did he come time enough to concert it; for the state of the War both by Sea and Land that year was fix'd before his arrival; which render'd it impossible for him to succeed in the Business he went about.

I shall not, I believe, need to repeat any Instances, that the States have always behav'd themselves with the utmost Respect to Her Majesty, and the Interest of Her People; when, to shew the true regard they have to any Proposition that shall come from her Britannick Majesty, after all this Ill treatment they consented to a *Congress* for Peace, even against their own Judgment, and that of their Allies, as is set forth in their Resolution upon that Subject. And after all the Clamour that is rais'd, they appear Guilty of nothing but of a little Prudent Management, the better to be enabled to bear the grievous Expences of so long a War; and not being able to answer all the parts of it, they let the Deficiency fall on their Fleet, where it wou'd be least felt, and the Service of the Common Cause least neglected. This is all the Conductor has to say against the *Dutch*, especially in relation to the Sea; and it is plain, they maintain above 140000 Men by Land, and the State of the War, for one Year, comes to near Four Millions and a half.

Besides which, 'tis necessary to observe, That the Revenue arising from the Places the *Dutch* are possess'd of in *Brabant* and *Flanders*, and of all the Places in the *Generality*, such as *Breda*, and others,

thers, that are not properly a part of the Seven Provinces; All this Revenue is appropriated to the Payment of Charges not within this Estimate. Each of the Seven Provinces a-part, is at the Charge of its own Civil Government; nor is there one of the Provinces that has not been oblig'd to borrow from time to time very great Sums to furnish their Contingent for the War; and consequently there is none of them that do not pay Annualy, a great deal for Interest, none of which Sums is reckon'd in this Estimate.

Now let the **Conducter** compare the Revenue of the Two Nations, with the Annual expence of each, and then see upon whom the weight of the War lies heaviest; and I dare engage it will be found that the *Dutch* lye under much heavier Pressures than our Selves: Which is at once a FULL ANSWER to all that has, or can be said against them. And if they were capable of being incens'd to desert their Allies, and going into the Interest of *France*, after having had the greatest hand in our Successes against them, he has furnish'd them with better Arguments to justifie their Proceedings, than any he has brought against them. And therefore to fall foul of them at so base a rate, is an instance of the utmost Ingratitude, when it rather ought to be the matter of Surprize, to consider the wonderful efforts they have made, in which they have out-done even the expectations of the Enemy; and I dare say, the Faction in *England*, are the only People in *Europe*, that do not think they have not done enough.

The **Conducter** having thus far attack'd the *Dutch*, he next falls foul on the late, and present Emperor, who 'tis necessary for his purpose likewise to bring into the List too; especially since he has Remonstrated against a Peace, which is sufficient alone to raise a Charge heavy enough against him. Passing by some few points that seem very trivial, I shall begin with a particular Complaint against the Emperor, under the Stile of the Imperial Court. *That instead of* 90000

Men, which they ought to furnish, neither of the two last Emperors, never had 20000 *on their own Account, but once in* Italy : Which is a Complaint just as true, as where he says, *There has not for some Years past been so many Men under the Duke of* Marlborough's *Command in* Flanders, *as the Queen alone maintains for that Service.* If I do not repeat the Words exactly, the Reader may turn a little back to the Quotation.

But to return : The Emperor we all know, did at the beginning of the War, certainly raise his full Quota of Troops ; and I dare say, that the *Corps* included in the Number, do still subsist, tho' the distant and hard Services they have been employ'd on, and the low Condition the Imperial Finances are reduc'd to by continual Wars, and the great Degree to which the Hereditary Countries are Exhausted of Men, have made it impossible for the late Emperors to Recruit them well. Once I think the Conducter allows the Imperial Court did exert themselves: And I must likewise affirm, That if they had not done it, the Liberty of *Europe* had been lost beyond a possibility of retrieving : This at least we owe to the Imperial Court, if we will but call to mind the prodigious Expence that first Campaign was to the Emperor, and what a Noble Body of Troops were destroy'd to make head, not only against the *French*, but the Duke of *Savoy*, and other Princes of *Italy* that join'd with the Enemy, which he held out for Six Campaigns, and with that Vigour and Success, as does sufficiently justifie the great zeal that was shewn to the Common Cause: And this I think the Conducter does not much deny, when he says, *That as soon as they had succeeded in their Attempt on the side of* Italy, *they found out the most effectual Expedient to excuse themselves.* And indeed, confessing, that after the Imperial Court had sustain'd the Burthen of the War in the most critical Place for Six years, it might with Reason be allow'd them to Breath a little : But then this was not till after the Battle of *Turin*, at which time, their

Affairs

Affairs were in the most desperate Condition. Neither after this Prodigious Success had set the Empire a little to rights, can it be said, *That they had succeeded in their Attempt on that side*; for as long as *Naples* remain'd in the Enemies Hands, it was impossible they shou'd be easie, and this made them exert themselves for one Campaign more at least; so that here were eight Campaigns before they had Succeeded, and were at leisure to find out the *Expedient* to excuse themselves: And for all the following Campaigns, 'tis known they had a considerable Number of Troops in *Flanders*, which the necessity of Affairs obliged them last year to draw away towards the *Rhine*. Besides which, 'tis known the Emperor has for several years past sent more than his Quota to the *Rhine*, as an example for other Princes to do the like. Nor did I ever hear that the Empire has been tax'd with neglect in furnishing their due Proportions to the Duke of *Savoy*; and if nothing has been done for these Four years past, it has not been for want of the Emperor's Troops to do their part, but from certain unlucky Disputes between him and the Duke of *Savoy*, which how far either side ought to have acquiesc'd in, is not my business to determine. Now, after having shewn all this, which is evident, even to the meanest Understanding that has but read the *Gazettes*; With what Justice or regard to Truth can it be affirm'd, *That neither of the late Emperors ever had* 20000 *Men on their own Account in the Common Cause?* Or wherein did they find *an Expedient*, but their inability to do more? which cannot be better shewn, than by the great Interest they pay here in *England*, for Mony borrow'd on the best Funds they have: It is with the same Justice that he says, (to cut with two edges, and wound the Duke of *M*——— at the same blow) *That they computed easily, it wou'd cost them less to make large Presents to one single Person, than to pay an Army*. What a ridiculous Assertion is this? especially after I have shewn, that they were not deficient in their Troops; And tho' I know the Duke does not want the assistance of so mean a Pen as mine to clear him from the Imputation of so Malicious a Suggestion; for indeed it is no more: I believe I may affirm, there is not in his whole Libel, (which is a bold word) so notorious a Falshood. I do confess indeed, That the First Emperor *Leopold*, in a just acknowledgment of his having preserv'd the Empire, made him a Prince thereof; an Honour which he several times declin'd, but at length, by repeated Intercessions, and with the Approbation of Her Majesty, he did accept it. And I think I have heard besides of a few Pictures given him, which having been the Elector of *Bavaria*'s, seem'd a very Natural and Decent Present to him who had freed the Empire from so dangerous an Enemy. More than these Presents I have never heard of any, and have just grounds to believe that he never receiv'd so much as one; and what is more, I do really believe the Conductor is of the same Opinion; which, if any thing can, adds to the Villiany of so base an Assertion.

Having thus in general complain'd of the two late Emperors, for not furnishing their *Quota's, and leaving it to us to fight their Battles*, He comes next particularly, to prove, *How little they regarded their Allies, when-ever they thought the Empire it self was Secure.* Now I wou'd fain know when that was, that the Empire was thought to be out of Danger? When it is otherwise very plain, that, after all the late Successes of the Imperial Court, it is not Secure yet; but is even at this time threaten'd with a new Invasion, if not oppos'd with more Vigour and Unanimity than hitherto has been shewn among the Princes of it; which easily shews us upon what mistaken Grounds the Conductor judges of things. We may remember how the Empire, as secure as it is said to be, (and was then, as far as any Thing I can see, as secure as it is now) was Ravag'd in the Year 1707, without almost any Opposition; and nothing is more certain, than that it had been

serv'd

serv'd so every Year since, had not the Duke of M——— by his admirable Vigilence, drawn the Enemies Attention another way, and oblig'd them to look to themselves instead of Invading others; so that they have often been compell'd to harrass their Troops by swift and troublesome Marches, to prevent some dreadful Blow in *Flanders*. We may, besides, with very good Reason, consider the Danger from the War in *Hungary* on one side, and of the just Apprehensions of an Insurrection in *Bavaria* on the other, where the least Spark, if not timely Extinguish'd, might have been very fatal to the Empire, especially while the *Hungarians* were in Arms. But we may easily see it is not the Empire the Conductor Quarrels with, who have been realy in Fault; but the Emperor, who has given no occasion at all, unless that he insists on the Restitution of *Spain*, which, as it is the Foundation of obstructing the Peace he Writes for, is sufficient to raise against him the most Partial Censure.

Another Complaint against him is, his not putting an end to the War in *Hungary, which* (says he) *he might have done several times upon Terms, not at all unbefitting either his Dignity or his Interest*. How far the Court of *Vienna* were to blame in this, does not appear by any instance the Conducter produces; and the Reasons there is to think, that if either of the Two late Emperors cou'd have put an end to that Dangerous War, on any Terms consistent with their Honour or Interest, make me believe it wou'd never have been omitted. Their Affairs were in the utmost Danger and Confusion both in *Italy* and the Empire, especially in 1707, when, as I have said, the Empire was Invaded. The King of *Sweden* was with a Victorious Army on the Frontiers, pressing into the Hereditary Dominions, and no Body knew what he design'd, or what wou'd content him; the Affairs of King *Charles* were at the same time at a Dangerous Crisis, and if these Necessities wou'd not

press

press them to put an end to such unhappy Troubles, it may very reasonably be thought, as all Governments are the best Judges of their own Affairs, that there was something which render'd it impossible to pacify them at that time; However, it can on no Construction be thrown on the late M——y, that they *tamely suffer'd the Emperor to Sacrifice the whole Alliance to his private Passion*, when it is so well known, that the M——rs of *England* and *Holland* labour'd indefatigably to carry this Point at *Vienna*; and what Pains the Earl of *S——d*, and Mr. *Stepney* particularly took in it; the former going thither expresly for that very purpose. Nor did ever any Men press a Thing more forcibly than the late M——rs did this Accomodation. So that tho' the Court of *Vienna* had been remiss, I cannot see where the Conducter can find room to throw the blame on the late M——y,

The next Complaint is the Affair of *Toulon*; which he draws in, to *shew the Emperor's indifference or dislike of the Common Cause*: The Miscarriage of which he throws wholly on the Court of *Vienna*. But first, as tho' he was infatuated to ruine the Credit of all he says, he tells you the Design was discover'd here by the *Creature* of a Great Man laying Wagers about the taking of it. This is a very odd way of proving that *Toulon* was lost, or rather not gain'd, by the Emperor's Neglect, to tell us first, that very probably it was not; for the Design was Discover'd here. *This Creature of a certain Great Man* happens to be known I believe, to very few People in *England*; but most Men can remember the Clerk of another Great Man who was diservedly Hang'd for something like it. One wou'd imagine by this, that his Arguments against the Emperor will be just as Wise; one of which is, That he had no mind *Toulon* shou'd be taken, because he dispatch'd 12000 Men to sieze *Naples*, as the Conducter ingeniously expresses it. Now, that the Emperor did at that time make an Expedition

pedition to *Naples*, is true, but not because he had no mind *Toulon* shou'd be taken; but in very deed, because those who wou'd make a Scandalous Peace now, were attempting the same thing then; which made him something more careful than ordinary to secure the Interest of his Family in *Italy*, where he had had a hard struggle to recover it, and was then afraid it wou'd have been Sacrific'd to other Views. This is the true State of this Matter, and not the Emperor's design, that the Siege of *Toulon* shou'd miscarry; nor did his Imperial Majesty, when he was press'd to put off this Expedition to *Naples*, want an Answer: He told them, That without these 12000 Men, they had as many as had been requir'd of him at first for the Expedition, which were more than wou'd be able to find Subsistance, wherefore more wou'd be but a Burthen to them; and while they were employ'd in the Reduction of *Toulon*, the other 12000 Men shou'd by great and speedy Marches hasten to *Naples*, and then return to join them for any farther Service.

Another Charge equally as just as this is, where he says, *That 'tis plain the Emperor had no mind* Toulon *shou'd be taken, because the Attempt might have succeeded if Prince* Eugene *had not thought fit to oppose it.* Now nothing is better known, than that the Duke of *Savoy* had the Chief Command in the Expedition; the Conducter had better have told us, if he cou'd, and very probable he did know, what was the Reason they delay'd their March so long; and after they had pass'd the *Var*, who it was that propos'd the holding a Council of War on Board the Fleet, to consider, whether to proceed directly to *Toulon*, or Besiege *Antibes*? From which step, and the time that was lost before, it was no hard matter to judge what was like to become of the Expedition. And again, let him resolve us, who Govern'd the Motions of the Army till they came before the Place? When the slowness of our Motions gave the Enemy an opportunity of possessing the High Grounds before our arrival, which was the true Reason of our Miscarriage there, and not the Fault of Prince *Eugene*, much less the Emperor, from whom, 'tis more than probable, by the great distance he was at, he had not time to receive fresh Instructions upon any sudden turn or prospect of Affairs: And if the Duke of *Savoy* did not think fit to hazard a Battle, it cou'd be no great Fault in Prince *Eugene*, that comply'd with him in drawing off the Army; but had the Expedition either been begun Ten Days sooner, or the March from the *Var* not so unaccountably delay'd, there is no doubt but the Design had Succeeded without the Troops dispatch'd to *Naples*, or running the risque of Attacking the Enemy in their strong Camp.

I shall only add to this, that be the Warlike Enterprizes adjusted as they will, it is in no wise chargeable on the late M——y, who form'd the Design with the greatest Secresy, and with the same Privacy made the most early and effectual preparations for the Execution of it; and as a farther and more particular effect of their Care and Concern therein, labour'd all they cou'd to divert the Design against *Naples*, and to remove any Difficulty that might possible be thought in the way to retard or prevent the Success of it.

Another Complaint against the late Emperor is indeed very extraoadinary; *That he drein'd into his own Coffers the Wealth of Countries Conquer'd or Recover'd for him by the War, without encreasing his Troops.* This is all over a very pleasant Banter, which sure the Conducter was not so Senceless to think cou'd pass upon the World, who know how full the Emperor's Coffers are like to be after so long a War, that were exhausted and empty even before it began. No doubt but his Successor, the present Emperor, wou'd be very glad to find the Truth of this; but I'm afraid he will only experience just the quite contrary.

But

But to see what this boasted Wealth arising from Conquer'd Countries must come to, we are to consider, the vast expense there must be in maintaining them after they are got. The best, and most considerable Persons generally remove themselves, and those that stay are to be gratified and kept in the Interest of the Conqueror, by such Favours as must diminish great part of the Revenues: There is likewise many times a necessity of remitting some considerable Duties, in regard of what the People have suffer'd by the War. This, with other incident Charges of taking strong Places, and maintaining them afterwards, may soon convince a Man of any Reason, how full the Emperor's Coffers are like to be: Were we to forget the Necessities the Empire has been put to for Money; and that even here we have a Mortgage upon the best, and most considerable Fund they have.

The next Part of the **Conducter**'s Charge against the Allies, is levied at the *Princes* of the *Empire*, of whom the Queen has hired Troops; yet the *Dutch* are so perpetually in his way, and the Design of lessening and defaming them being his chief aim, he lets fall some of his Malice and Virulence by the way: *In order to augment our Forces*, says he, *every year, in the same proportion as those for whom we fight diminish theirs, we have been oblig'd to hire from several Princes of the Empire.* To shew the falsity of this, and how liable the **Conducter** is to prevaricate when his Purpose is to be serv'd by it; he is so far mistaken, as that we did not begin to hire, in order to Augment our Forces: Our first 40,000 Men, were for the most part compos'd of hir'd Troops, to save *English* Blood, and that there might lye the fewer on the Nation to provide for at the end of the War. Now these Forces we have not augmented every year; and when ever we did augment our Troops in *Flanders*, the States, as I have already shewn, did equally augment theirs; so far were they from diminishing

minishing their Troops from Time to Time; and much less cou'd the Proportion in which they diminish'd their Troops, be the Rule by which we encreas'd ours, as the Conducter endeavours to shew; nor is it for them we Fight, but for our selves; the common concern and safety of us all. But he proceeds, and says, *The Ministers of which Princes, have perpetually importun'd the Court, with unreasonable demands, under which our late M——rs were Passive.* Here he includes all the Princes; but I must tell him that one of them at least has not been importuniate *with unreasonable Demands*, and that is the Elector of *Hanover*, to name no others; Nor have the rest been perpetually so unreasonable as he makes, tho' it must be confess'd they were always for making the best Bargain they cou'd; which however does not affect the late M——y, when it can be prov'd, that they have many times oblig'd them to desist from their first Pretensions; and many have been utterly refus'd. But what is worse —— says he, *These Demands were always back'd with a Threat to recall their Troops; which was a Thing not to be heard of, because it might disoblige the Dutch.*

Were this true, (which by the way, has been more since the admission of the new M——y than the beginning of the War besides) it has been chiefly under pretense, that they were oblig'd so to do, in respect to their own safety; unless the Allies wou'd concur with their Remonstrances to secure the Peace of the Empire, and oblige the King of *Sweden* to a Neutrality: Whatever was the particular occasion, the Treaties for their Troops are but for a year only, and when they are to be renew'd, they are at liberty to insist on new Articles; and if they grow upon us in their Demands, 'tis because they are of great Service to us, and that the War is more our concern than theirs. And if the recalling their Troops is a thing not to be heard of, 'tis not because it might disoblige the *Dutch*, but because

both

both we and the *Dutch* want them; and because the *Dutch* hire Troops of the same Princes as well as we, and are oblig'd many times to submit to the same unreasonable Demands; the doing of which is of such Consequence, that a stop must be put else to the Progress of our Arms, and the Fruits of a promising Campaign lost, by hiring a good Body of Troops recall'd in the middle of it: Which we had like to have experienc'd last Year, had not the Duke of *M*—— found out an Expedient to prevent it, without submitting to any unreasonable Demand. But after these, and other frivolous accusations against these Princes, I wou'd come to the main point, and know, Whether this is to be charg'd upon any of our Principal Allies? Much less upon the late M——y? Is it not well known that the Emperor himself can't redress this? And that the Fault lies in Constitution of the Empire, there not being any sufficient Power vested in't, to oblige these Princes to Contribute as they ought to the Defence of it, the Quota's they are assess'd by the *Diet*, tho' that *Diet* be themselves, and the Resolutions of it consequently their own Acts.

The next complaint against these Princes, carries with it so impudent a Reflection, as I am confident is not to be presidented in any Book ever Printed, where the Characters of Princes in Alliance with us, are drawn in such odious and villainous Colours, as nothing can excuse it; and the Honour and Justice of Nations, especially our own, are so infamously perverted, as must needs be shocking to all that have any sence of the Dignity sacred to Crown'd Heads. The Charge against them, being a general Character of all the Princes to whom we pay Subsidies, in the Terms following: *There is hardly*, (says he) *a Petty Prince to whom we pay Subsidies and Pensions, who is not ready upon every occasion to threaten us to recall their Troops, (tho they must ROB or STARVE at Home) if we refuse to comply with him in Demand, however so unreasonable,*

Is

Is not this very pretty Language to treat Crown'd Heads with? And shou'd not the Elector of *Hanover* have been excus'd at least? Is this villainous and infamous Treatment fit for Crown'd Heads? Princes that are our Friends, in the same Interest, and of the same Religion with us? For under this Title, *of Petty Princes*, are meant, and principally included, the Kings of *Denmark*, *Prussia* and *Poland*. Notwithstanding any prevarication the **Conducter** since makes, the first ought to expect better Treatment, both as a Protestant, and an old Ally; if not out of a sence of his particular Relation to her Majesty. The second, has been a very zealous and hearty promoter of the Common Cause, and of the Protestant Religion, his Purse and his Country are always liberally open to Poor Refugees; and nothing is omitted by him, which may possibly contribute to Enlarge the Reform'd Religion. And even the last, tho' it will always be a blemish to him, that he parted with his Religion for the Possession of a Crown, yet amidst all his troubles, he has appear'd with great firmness in the Interest of the Grand Alliance; whilst his Insulting and Victorious Enemy the King of *Sweden*, instead of assisting with his necessary Quota, unnaturally forc'd the Emperor by Threats, and a dishonourable Treaty, to desist from all Demands therein, past, present, and to come, till he had ended the War he was engag'd in; and what more was fear'd from him, made this, as well as some other hard Articles, be agreed to by the Court of *Vienna*. These are some of the Princes that are to ROB or STARVE if it were not for our Subsidies; which Assertion is beyond all Truth, Honesty, or Good Manners.

But cou'd this infamous Charge against them be suppos'd to have any thing in it of Truth, I wou'd once more fain know of the **Conducter**, how he proves his Point, *That our Allies have broke every Article of their Treaty with us?* Or whether the Faults they are Charg'd with, come within the Terms of Establish'd Treaties, but are rather generally the effects of

[illegible]

new Engagements, and not proceeding from any Disregard to the Queen, or Neglect of the Common Cause; but for the most part from their general Weakness, or an Inability to do otherwise; or perhaps from the Difficulty or Necessity of their Affairs at some particular Junctures. And in the second place, were these Princes inexcusable in their Conduct and Behaviour, as to their Parts in the War, Is it an Argument that *the late M——y have suffer'd it?* When it is so well known, what Methods they have taken to make them exert themselves in the most effectual Manner? what Remonstrances and Expostulations they have us'd? which were sufficiently back'd by the Ministers of the States, who with the same Force and Vigour always press'd the Service of the Common Cause, where-ever they found any of their Allies defective. But if after all this assiduity, some Faults have remain'd in any of our Allies, and all Parts have not done, what by the Tenour of their Treaties they were oblig'd to, Is there any thing in it so very wonderful? Was there ever any Alliance where it was otherwise? or is it possible to suppose there ever will? And is it not rather matter of the greatest Wonder and Reflection, That a Confederacy consisting of so many different Forms of Government, and no less different Interests, shou'd subsist so many years with that Harmony it has done? and be render'd so Successful against a very formidable Enemy? Nor have their Artifices in so long a War, (where doubtless no Endeavours were omitted) been able to corrupt the least of them by any Offers into separate Measures; which I believe is without Example, and which we must never hope to see again, if the Conducter and his Friends carry their Point in view. And is it not easie to imagine the mighty Advantage the *French* have in this particular, who are a single Power, and have all Orders within themselves; and may with a greater dispatch and secrecy bring all the Parts of the War to bear, whilst in a Confederacy, consisting of so many different and Independant Powers, it is impossible to act with that vigour and unanimity that is requisite: And if the Alliance has succeeded under these, and many the like Inconveniencies, is there not the greater ground to take of all Censure from the late M--y, and give 'em the undoubted Praises due to their great Abilities, Prudence, and Integrity.? who by the Influence their dext'rous Councils have had in Forreign Courts, have chiefly contributed to keep so extensive an Alliance so long in Harmony and Concert; by which alone, in all humane possibility, they have been able to humble so formidable an Enemy. And if no Alliance must be made, or kept up, till such little Inconveniencies, as these objected, can be overrul'd, 'tis in vain ever to think of making any; but to give all up, and submit to the Common Enemy, which perhaps is the **Conducter**'s sence of future Benefits.

It will be needless to argue farther on this Point, since what is urg'd by the *Adversary* has so little of moment in it; but more especially, because it does not come up to the Propositions laid down, *That either the Allies have broke all their Treaties*; or that if they had, *it is chargeable on the late M — y*, both which Points were chiefly his view: But that no Invective may be spar'd where he can find an opportunity to bring it in, he now takes the new Emperor to Task, for 'tis something necessary to his Purpose to render him too as odious as he can. *The whole Army in Catalonia*, says he, *which is, or ought to be* 50000 *Men, exlusive of* Portugal *and* Gibraltar, *is paid by the Queen, excepting only Seven Battalions, and Fourteen Squadrons, of* Dutch *and* Palatines; *and even* 1500 *of these in our Pay*; *besides the Subsidies to King* Charles. But it is observable he do's not in this Number include the *Spaniards*, who have constantly been paid out of the Subsidy, and never receiv'd a Farthing out of any other Money. He infers that the

the Queen paid about 43000 Men, out of 50000; which how true it is, the Reader may see by the exact Abstract of all the Forces that have been yearly paid by Her Majesty, or provided for by Parliament, for the Service of *Catalonia*, or to act on that side since the War began there, which was in 1705. exclusive of *Portugal*, and besides the Subsidies granted the King of *Spain*: For the Year 1705. ending at *Christmas*, 4970 Men. For the Year 1706, 18757 Men; in which Number is included, 5330 Men, which the Parliament provided for, to Serve in other Parts, *viz.* One Regiment in *Portugal*, Four in *Flanders*, and a Battalion of Guards on the Establishment of Guards and Garrisons. For the Year 1707. the Troops provided for to Serve in *Spain* and *Portugal* were 29395 Men, of which the Corps that Serv'd in *Spain*, exclusive of *Gibraltar*, if compleat, according to their Establishment, wou'd make 25141 Men; and adding the Battalion of Guards and Marines, amount to 27141. Of this Number Six Regiments of Foot were reduc'd, and the Officers sent Home to Recruit in *March* 170⅞. For the Year 1708. of the Troops provided for to Serve in *Portugal*, and other Parts, there serv'd in *Catalonia* 17910 Men. But the Numbers Voted for this Year to Serve in *Spain*, and other Parts, were 30530 Men: Of which 12620 Serv'd in *Portugal*, *Gibraltar*, *Great-Britain*, and on the Expedition under General *Erle*. For the Year 1709. Of the Troops provided to Serve in *Spain*, *Portugal*, and elsewhere, there Serv'd on the side of *Catalonia*, including 3800 *Portugueze*, to which Number they were then reduc'd from 7000 Men, 32644; towards whose Pay the Queen gave 80000 *l.* For the Year 1710. Of the Troops granted for *Spain* and elsewhere, there Serv'd on the side of *Catalonia*, including the Garrisons of Port *Mahone*, and the 3800 *Portugueze*, 33995. For the Year 1711. 32900 Men. But several Regiments taken at *Bribuega*, the latter end of the Year 1710. continuing still Prisoners, are not included here, altho' provided for to serve in *Catalonia*. Now the Subsidies granted to the King of *Spain*, were every year thus: For 1706, 103000 *l.* For 1707, 150000. For 1708, 150000. For 1709, 150000. For 1710, 150000. And for 1711, 150000. Out of which was defray'd, besides paying the *Spanish* Troops, the Charge of Fortifications, (omitting Port *Mahone*, and *Gibraltar*) with the Charge of Subsisting great Numbers of *Spaniards* at *Lisbon*, and elsewhere, as they deserted from the Enemy, pursuant to the Manifesto of the *English* General; and some other Heads of Expence; by which it may be imagin'd what great Number of Troops cou'd be kept with the Remainder.

Immediately after which the **Conducter** alledges, *That we were at the whole Charge of Transporting all the Troops from* Italy, *and paid Levy-Money for every individual Man and Horse*; which may pass for another Equivocation; For we never Paid the Transportation of one Man or Horse, except such as were actually in the Queen's Pay. As for the *Dutch*, they constantly paid the Charge of Transporting the Troops in their own Pay. And as to the Levy-Money, there never was one Farthing paid for the Horse. The Allowance was 5 *l.* for every effective Man that shou'd be actually Embark'd; and it was only for the Imperial Regiments, none at all being paid for the *Italians*, *Neopolitans*, or *Grisons*; and if we had paid for Man and Horse, as he infers, it wou'd have come to 20 *l.* at least.

A Page or two farther he says, *That Seven* Portugueze *Regiments, after the Battle of* Almanza, *went off with the rest of that broken Army to* Catalonia; *the King of* Portugal *said he was not able to pay them while they were out of his Country; the Queen consented therefore to do it Her self, provided that King wou'd raise as many more to supply their Room. This he engag'd to do, but never perform'd. Notwithstanding which, his Subsidies*

dies were constantly paid him by my Lord G———; for almost four Years, without any Deduction upon Account of these seven Regiments. Of all which, there is not a true syllable: Of these Seven Regiments he speaks of; Five of them were Horse, and the other Two Foot, which when compleat, amounted to 134707 *l.* 5 *s.* 4 *d.* ¾ *per Annum*. This was entirely born by the King of *Portugal* to the first of *December* 1708. But having in the year 1709. rais'd a new Army, and the Expence of these seven Regiments encreasing greatly by the Extraordinary Charge of furnishing Money, Provisions, and other Necessaries to them, in a Country where the Court of *Lisbon* had but a slender Credit; The Q—— n, to Ease the growing Charge, consented to pay 80000 *l.* towards their Pay, for the Year 1709. They were paid about the like Sum for the Years 1710, and 1711, and receiv'd Subsistance for their Effectives, in like manner as the other Troops. And from the end of *December* 1708; to which time the Q—— n did not expend one Groat for the Seven Regiments before-mentioned, to the end of *August* 1710. (which was the last Months Subsidy the King of *Portugal* ever receiv'd in my Lord T—— r's time) is Twenty Months, which the Conducter tells us with Assurance is four Years. And notwithstanding what he says, *That the King of* Portugal *rais'd no Forces in the room of the Seven Regiments:* He knows that the *Portugal* Minister, upon enquiry into this Affair about a Twelve Month ago, gave the Court entire Satisfaction to the contrary. Nor is he ignorant, that in the Year 1708. there was 25000 *l.* paid out of the Treasury for part of the Subsidy for buying Horses here, to remount the King of *Portugal*'s Cavalry, which was expended accordingly; and the Horses were Transported at his own proper Charge, and the Money was deducted out of the Subsidy due to him: Which Sum alone is almost sufficient to Mount the Four or Five Regiments of Horse aforesaid.

 Ano-

Another Objection he has in this Point: He intimates, *That we have been put to double Expence in maintaining our Troops by the Charge of Forage*: Which has much the same air of Truth and Ingenuity, with what has gone before. The Army in *Portugal*, as well those in the King of *Portugal*'s Pay, as those upon Her Majesty's Establishment, are furnish'd by Contracts made with *English* Merchants, and Factors. The Corn they use is for the most part of the Product of *Great Britain* and *Ireland*; and the Rates agreed upon by Contract, is regulated according to the Price of Corn in the Markets of *Lisbon*; which of late years has been so high, that it was difficult many times to get the Contracts compleated; in-somuch, that for a Year, beginning at *Michaelmas* 1710. there was such an Advance, in the Price agreed upon, that the Ration of Bread or Forrage ran at a greater Rate than the Soldiers cou'd allow for it out of their Subsistence, and therefore the Overplus became a Charge to the Government, and consequently occasion'd an Expence to the Q—— n for that Year of 5000 *l*. The Contract for the next Year 1711. extended to an higher Price; so that the extraordinary Charge to the Q——n, wou'd have amounted to 30000, provided the Troops there had been Compleat, according to their Establishments: But as there are many Regiments already reduc'd, and others drawn off, this extraordinary Charge will not amount to 10000 *l*. a Sum very far short of double the Charge of Maintaining our Troops, as this Ingenuous Writer injuriously affirms. And to shew how little Interest the King of *Portugal* has in this Extraordinary Expence by these Contracts, wherein he bears much the greatest share in supplying his own Troops, it is certainly known, that when this Affair was taken notice of here, the *Portugal* Envoy presented a Memorial to Her Majesty, requiring, or rather proposing, that she would be pleas'd to give Directions for Furnishing Her Troops in *Portugal*

with

with Bread and Forrage by Comissaries, or Contracters, of her own Appointment; in which case they might make the best Terms they cou'd for Her Majesty's Advantage: And the chief Reasons he gave were, That the Court of *Portugal* found it very difficult to get Persons to Enter into such Contracts, tho' at much higher Rates than usual, and by which, instead of Advantage, nothing but loss cou'd accrue to His *Portugueze* Majesty.

I have been led something out of the way by the Author's very singular Method of Writing, who, as he is never weary of saying the same thing over and over, so his Arguments are scatter'd and interspers'd throughout the whole Libel, as make it impossible, if it were not unnecessary, to Answer them in any regular manner. He cannot well forget his old Friends the *Dutch*, and that he may not leave any thing unsaid to brand them with as much Infamy as is possible, he now draws them into a Confederacy with the Duke of *M*—— in fleecing and oppressing the People of the *Netherlands*. *The Hollanders*, says he, *have made good use of their time, and in Conjunction with our G*——*l, the oppressions of* Flanders *are much greater than ever*. Now if there were one word of Truth in this, I wou'd forgive all he has said; I wonder we were not told the particulars of these *Oppressions*, what they were, and in what manner they have been redress'd by the New M——y? There is no dispute, had there been any thing of Fact in it, that the Conducter cou'd not, thro' the Interest of his Friends, have wanted due Intelligence; and how much the proving of this Assertion wou'd have contributed to the serving of a *Purpose*, is sufficient to convince me it did not want for Industry to find it out. This is indeed the true True Reason why People are not told in what manner the Duke of *M*—— Oppress'd those Provinces; and it is for the same Reason that they did not impeach his Favourite C——n, tho' they went as far in using him ill as they well cou'd, and wou'd not have bated so material an Article as this, if it cou'd have done him any harm, or themselves any good. But the Truth is, it wou'd not; the Oppressions he speaks of, where only necessary points of Justice, and transacted conformable to the most solemn Councils, and all the Rules of War. And to shew that they were so, it is to be observ'd, that since the year 1708, when Prince *Eugene* join'd my Lord *M*—— with a Body of Imperial Troops, besides a few Regiments rais'd and maintain'd by this Country, they have found Bread and Forrage for these Troops. And to answer this Charge, and other necessary Expences of the War, the yearly Revenue of these Provinces not being sufficient, they borrow'd Money upon some Branches of it, to support the Service; none of which were engag'd for above Ten Years, and some not above Four or Five. This is the wonderful Oppression these People have lain under; they have paid what was necessary for their own Defence, and what cou'd not, without the greatest injustice to other People, be dispens'd with. I wou'd ask the **Conducter** which way the War cou'd have been carried on with the Success it has been, without these Troops? Or if this, either thro' Folly or Obstinacy, cou'd be objected to, which way they shou'd otherwise have been maintain'd? Was it requisite that the Emperor shou'd have been at that Expence? Who declares, That tho' Bread and Forrage are found for these Troops of his, they are a greater Charge to him than if they had serv'd on the *Rhine*. Was it Reasonable, that the Queen or the States, shou'd have paid this additional Charge? Because in other places he says, *The burden of the War was too heavy for us before*; and if it was upon us, I can answer it was so upon the *Dutch*: There is therefore no place it cou'd fall on, so justly as these Provinces: And is there any Reason they shou'd be exempted from the Charge, or have their Revenues kept clear, when those of most of the Con-

Confederates are so much anticipated? Not only that they are the most easie in this point, but that they have also the least Reason to complain of all People, in regard that by the assistance of these Troops, the Duke of *M*——— has been chiefly enabled to carry the Seat of the War out of their Provinces, where they must have suffer'd more in one Campaign by the Ravages of Two Powerful Armies, than all the other Methods that have been us'd of Subjugating them to pay a little Money for their Quiet, under the dreadful Name of OPPRESSIONS; forgetting otherwise the great Advantages they enjoy by having great Summs of Money continually Circulating thro' their principal Towns, where they find the Army a ready Market for the Produce of their Country, and at least reap this Benefit, of Paying their Subsidies in the way of Trade, and not in Specie, which they have a treble return for. And is it not to the Conduct and Vigilance of the Duke of *M*——, that they owe these Advantages, and of living free from the Inconveniencies and Ravages of an Army? Besides, is it not the Troops of their Natural and Lawful Prince they pay these Subsidies of Bread and Forrage to, whose Interest, as well as their own Preservation, is owing to the Success of the War? And is not this more than a single Reason why they shou'd Contribute their share to it? Nor were it any hard matter to shew, if I have not sufficiently done it already, that the Duke of *M*——— instead of oppressing these Provinces, has been their greatest Benefactor; No one instance of Oppression being by any of these Provinces Personally imputed to him. To prevaricate therefore, 'tis pretended that *M*—— C——n had done it under his Protection, and for his Interest. But as I have observ'd before, if either of these cou'd be prov'd, there is nothing more certain, than that it had not been omitted till now; but brought under the general Cognizance of Complaints; nothing of which has appear'd more groundleſs, than the Clamours rais'd againſt the Duke of *M*—— on this occaſion, or can we yet ſee the great Summs of Money they tell us have been miſapply'd, which have been ſo ſtrongly buzz'd into the Heads of the People. But further yet, I will undertake to prove, That *M*—— C—— n has not Oppreſs'd theſe Provinces, nay that he cou'd not do it; it being too well known, That neither he, nor the States Deputies, who are call'd a *Conference*, ever touch'd a Penny of the Publick Mony. Their Buſineſs was to repreſent to the *Council of State*, what Summs the ſeveral Branches of the Service wou'd require, and by ſome reaſonable Method, oblige them to think of complying with the Demands. But after this, they had no further Hand in it, the Money was Levied and Collected, and Iſſu'd by their own particular Orders, never once coming under the Diſpoſal of *M*—— C——n, or the States Deputies, ſo that it was impoſſible any Fraud or Oppreſſion cou'd be carried on by Them. They often found it difficult to make a *Council of State* do what was neceſſary for carrying on the Service; which oblig'd the *Conference* ſometimes to be round with them, and to let them underſtand, that they had demanded nothing but what was abſolutely requiſite to be comply'd with. They have ſometimes likewiſe over-rul'd the *Council of State*, in the buſineſs of Chuſing their Magiſtrates: And ſince the Surprize of *Ghent*, which every Body knows was the effect of Treachery, they have found it neceſſary to intermeddle in an Affair of that Conſequence, which diſcover'd too plainly the Diſpoſition of thoſe Provinces to favour the *French* or *Bavarian* Intereſt. If theſe were Oppreſſions, theſe Provinces have Reaſon of complaint; and that they have Suffer'd till the laſt Year, which has given them all the Relief they cou'd expect or deſire; for inſtead of finding Bread and Forrage for this Body of Imperial Troops, the laſt Campaign they refus'd to provide for one ſingle Regiment of *Huſſars*, which

which Prince *Eugene* was prevail'd with to leave behind him; the Service at that time being in great want of them. Nor was the least thing the Duke of *M*—— ask'd of them comply'd with, but with the greatest difficulty imaginable. Their Disaffection to the Common Cause, was so apparant, that toward the end of the Campaign, when the Army found it difficult to subsist in the Neighbourhood of *Bouchain*, they refus'd the Duke of *M*—— a supply of Forrage; notwithstanding it was represented to them in the most pressing manner, that such a refusal cou'd only be attended with the return of the Army into those Provinces; yet they sent a Deputation to the Army, desiring to be excus'd, and delay'd it so long, that our Troops Suffer'd greatly by their Willful Neglect, tho' the Duke found means to subsist them longer than cou'd be expected. This is the happy Change they have receiv'd in their Affairs. They have likewise been Reliev'd in the point of Chusing their Magistrates; and the good use they have made of this Liberty, is, that they have put the very Persons into the Magistracy of *Ghent*, that are suspected of having before Betray'd it to the *French*; nor wou'd it be any Surprize, if we shou'd hear the same again. Their other Towns are fill'd with Persons of the same Faction, and from whom, when opportunity serves, we may expect the same faithless Dealings. This is the true State of the Duke of *M* ——'s Oppressing these Provinces in Conjunction with the *Dutch*, and of the Benefits we are like to have by their Relief.

Honour, I find the **Conducter** has a very barbarous and contemptible Notion of, and seems to think at least, that in the Beggerly condition he has represented his Country, we have no occasion to stand much on that point. *It will no doubt*, says he, *be a mighty comfort to our Grand-Children, when they see a few Rags hang up in* Westminster-Hall, *which cost an Hundred Millions, whereof they are paying the Ar-*

rears,

rears, and boasting, as Beggars do, that their Grand-Fathers were Rich and Great. There is something in these *Rags*, that the **Conducter** cannot endure to think of; every little Motion the Air gives them, bespeaks the Honour of that unequall'd Man who plac'd them there; and will do so to all Posterity, as long as any signs of them shall remain: But *Rags* they are, he says, and *Rags* e'en let 'em be, they were thought of the more Honour in the Hands of those they were taken from, and will be so were they are, whilst there is History to relate the incredible Successes of those Days; That *Britain* Tryumph'd over her Enemies, in so many Glorious Emblems of her Memorable and Repeated Conquests! And 'tis with a Heavy Heart I Wish, our Grand-Children have not rather Cause by that Time, to Mourn the real Miseries which the Tenets of this Destructive Book may bring on them, and Reflect what a Flourishing State their Ancestors were in, when they were so compleatly blest with Liberty and Conquest, which the Antiquity of those *Rags*, if they are still suffer'd to remain there, will give them a Melancholly, but true Idea of.

Having thus sported with these *Rags*, as he Terms them, the use he makes of it is this, *that after all these Miraculous Doings, we are not yet in a Condition to bring* France *to our Terms, nor can tell when we shall.* I wish the **Conducter** and his Friends, wou'd be persuaded to put this upon the Issue of a fair Tryal, and leave *France* to shift for her self, I shou'd be far from making the least doubt *of bringing Them to our Terms.* But he Writ before the Allies had given in their Demands to the Offers of *France*, and therefore may be excus'd: And I will further affirm, That if we do not now *bring* France *to our Terms*, it must be owing to the Conversation they have had with his Book, which perhaps may have intoxicated them, and turn'd their Heads; but if they remain in their Sences, and find no Encouragement *Elsewhere*, 'tis easie

easie to conclude we shall soon have a better Peace than the Conducter Writes for; and at once destroy another Argument he makes use of —— *That our Victories only serv'd to lead us on to farther Visionary Prospects; where Romantick Views were propos'd, and the old reasonable sober Design was forgot*, by which he means the Restitution of *Spain* and the *Indies*; nor know I of any *further Visionary Prospects, or Romantick Views*. The Restitution of *Spain* and the *Indies*, was always the point in View, and 'tis very strange that any Reasonable or Sober Man shou'd say otherwise; to which End the Grand Alliance was expresly form'd, in opposition to the Partition Treaty that the Emperor so much dislik'd; and in all the overtures made by *France*, this was always made the first Preleminary, constantly laid down by all the Allies, and never Disputed by the Enemy: But thinking to help the Enemy out a little, he says, *That the Face of Affairs, since the Emperor's death, has been very much chang'd*. True, they have so, but not in his sence, they have chang'd much for the better on the Confederates side, not on the side of *France*. The Accession of King *Charles* to the Imperial Throne, has put it in his own Power to assert his Right to the Crown of *Spain* with more vigour than ever, and what he was fain to Solicit, in vain sometimes, from a Father or a Brother, he may now Command; and possibly with a double chearfulness from his Subjects. But such a Union of the two Crowns in the House of *Austria*, is of late render'd in dreadful Colours; it may indeed be so to *France*, but to no body else, at least not to *England*, whose Fleets the Emperor will always have occasion for, to render *Spain* and the *Indies* useful to him, which must needs be attended with some very great Advantage on our side. But he tells us, *That the* Dutch *like this Union as little as any Body, whatever they may now pretend, and resolv'd those two Powers shou'd not be join'd in the same Person*. The

Con-

Conductor ſhou'd have ſhewn us this Reſolution of the *Dutch*, if he wou'd have us believe him. 'Tis poſſible that the ſudden and unexpected Death of the late Emperor a little ſtartled them; and as Things then ſtood, before they cou'd well recollect themſelves, they might be drawn in to liſten to a kind of Scheme in Favour of the Duke of *S——y*; which as ſoon as they had well conſider'd, they found that Duke had no Claim, by any Pretence, to the *Spaniſh* Dominions, till after the Demiſe of King *Charles*; whoſe Election to the Imperial Dignity, cou'd no way obſtruct his Right to *Spain*. But ſuppoſe it had been otherwiſe, wou'd ſuch a Project in favour of the Duke of *S——y* have any ways mended the matter? Wou'd *France* be more willing he ſhou'd have the Monarchy of *Spain* than the Emperor? Or was he in a better Condition to maintain his Petenſions to it? Nay, ſuppoſe the Allies had declar'd for him, cou'd he have made any other uſe of it, but to have Exchang'd it with *France* for an Equivalent in *Italy*? Where nothing cou'd have been given him but in Prejudice of the Emperor, who had redeem'd what he had there by the Sword, and at immenſe Charge. How then wou'd ſuch a Scheme have reduc'd the *Exorbitant* Power of *France*, or excluded them from the Trade of the *Indies?* Which is ſo ſtrongly ſtipulated for by the Grand Alliance, and is above all moſt particularly the concern of *Britain*. Theſe were ſome of the Reaſons that made the States utterly reject the Project in favour of *S——y*. And that is one Reaſon perhaps we are ſo angry with them, and ſo fond of the Duke of *S——y*, againſt whom we hear no Complaints, tho' his Conduct for theſe Four Campaigns paſt, wou'd otherwiſe have made ſome very ſhining Paragraphs in this Libel.

So

So much of the Conducter's Malice is levied at the *Dutch*, that they are constantly brought in let the Scene lye where it will. *Thus they put the late King upon spending Six Millions a year to enlarge their Frontiers; They got all the Advantages of the* Reswick Treaty; *and have been Insolent, Unjust, and Ingrateful in This: The* Dutch *might have Defended themselves with the* 10000 *Men King* William *sent them, without involving us in the Rupture.* And then Ten Thousand to One but we had been by this time, in the Condition the Conducter wou'd have us. *The enlarging the* Dutch *Frontiers is of no real solid Advantage to us; And that 'tis an affront and lessening to us, to couple us with them, and call us jointly the Maratime Powers.* Contrary to what we have from that Great and Learned Author Sir *Walter Rawleigh*; who says, *That he shall never think him a Lover of his King and Country, that shou'd persuade His Majesty from embracing the Amity of the States of* Holland; *His Majesty being no less safe by them, than they invincible by him. The* Dutch *have broke their Alliances; and the* Dutch *design to rob us of our Manufactures, to encrease their own Trade and Strength; The* Dutch *bubbled us with the Guarantee of our Succession.* In Answer to this heap of Scandal, and many other as vile Assertions as these, I think it proper to let the Reader see, if he can find one any of the Facts they are Charg'd with in the following Letter; such as *Treachery, Insolence, Injustice, Ingratitude, Baseness, Theft, &c.* which coming to my Hands just as this Sheet was in the Press, has furnish'd me with an opportunity of stopping the Conducter's Mouth, from the Undeniable instances of Honour and Respect, that the States have always paid to Her Majesty; and is a *Full Answer* to all that has been objected against them; and indeed, to any other unjust Complaint that the *French* Faction can raise against them.

The

The Representation of the States General to the Court of *Great Britain*, by a LETTER dated *Feb.* 19. 1712. *N. S.*

THat during the whole Course of her Majesty's Glorious Reign, they have had nothing more at Heart, than to cultivate and maintain with Her a good Friendship, perfect Confidence and Union, and to corroborate them the most they possibly could; having always judged them absolutely necessary, and especially in the present Conjuncture. That they likewise judged they could not give a better Proof of this their Disposition and Perswasion, than that which they lately gave, in agreeing to the Proposition which her Majesty had caused to be made to them, to begin the Negociation of a General Peace with the Enemy, and in concurring with her Majesty to facilitate the bringing together of the Ministers of all the High Allies to the Congress at Utrecht. *That they are perswaded nothing can more contribute to the Dispatch and Success of that Negociation, than a strict Union and intire Harmony between her Majesty and their State. That as they had the Honour to conclude with her Majesty the 29th of* Octob. *1709, the Treaty of mutual Guarantie, commonly called the Barrier Treaty, ratified on both Sides in the most Authentick Form, They looked upon it not only as a Foundation of their own Safety, for securing which they entered into the present War and have carried it on so many Years, but likewise as a firm Support of that good Understanding and Union between Her Majesty and their State, which they so earnestly and sincerely desire to see continued; so that they could never doubt in any Manner, that they should not at all times enjoy the Effect of the said Treaty. That however, having not long since been inform'd, that in* England *some were of Opinion that the said Treaty in some Articles might be prejudicial to Her Majesty's Subjects, they commission'd M.* Buys *their Envoy extraordinary, then going to* England, *to enquire what*

what those Points were, that might be thought Grievances, and authoris'd him to treat about them, with Her Majesty's Ministers, and to remove, if possible, the Difficulties by all the Explanations that should appear necessary; which they were put in Hopes would not be very hard to do, when once they should have consented to concur with Her Majesty, as they did, to procure a Congress for the Negociation of a General Peace. *But the Misfortune was, that the said M.* Buys, *during his Residence in* England, *was not able to finish that Affair to reciprocal Satisfaction; and that it having been remitted to the* Hague, *no way has hitherto been found to terminate it there neither; tho' their High Mightinesses think they have shewn all the Readiness to comply with any just Expedient, that could reasonably be expected from them; For, having learnt that the principal Exceptations taken to the said Treaty, were, that it might prove prejudicial to the Commerce of Her Majesty's Subjects in the* Spanish Netherlands, *and that some had entertained an ill-grounded and erroneous Opinion, that the States might design to take Advantage by it, to make themselves Masters of the said* Spanish Netherlands; *their High Mightinesses did declare positively, and by this Letter do voluntarily repeat it, that it never was their Intention, nor ever will be, to make use of the said Treaty, or of their Garrisons in the fortified Places of the Country, to prejudice in any manner the Commerce of Her Majesty's Subjects; but that their Opinion is, That whatever relates to Navigation and Commerce there, ought to be settled on an intire Equality, that so Her Majesty's Subjects may not be charg'd with higher Duties of Importation or Exportation than theirs, to the End Commerce may be carried on there by both Nations on an equal Foot. That their High Mightinesses did declare, and do declare again by this Letter, That they never had a Thought, nor have now, of making themselves Masters of the* Spanish Netherlands *in whole, or in part; con-*

renting themselves to have Garrisons in the Places mentioned in the 6th Article, with the Revenues specified in the 11th Article, and what is stipulated by the others separate from the said Treaty. That besides, they have not the least Thought of making use of the Priviledge stipulated in the 7th Article to put Troops into other Places, but only in case of the last and most apparent Necessity. That they hope by this positive Declaration, to have the Happiness to remove all those Suspicions which may wrongfully have been conceived against them; and that they have firm Confidence in her Majesty's so renowned Equity, that she will not do any thing in Prejudice of the said Treaty, nor permit any to be done to it; but rather that she will be pleased to see that they may have the intire Effect of it, and take off all Uneasiness they may be in about it; which they most earnestly desire of Her Majesty. Adding, That if there be some Articles of the said Treaty, which without affecting the Essentials of it, may be thought to want Explanation, Her Majesty shall find them willing and ready to treat thereupon, and with all the Facility and Condescension that can reasonably be required of them, without doing Prejudice to the Rights they have acquired, not only by the said Treaty, but by other preceeding ones; and in whatever shall not be of the last Importance for the Security and Preservation of their State. They conclude, with intreating Her Majesty to continue towards them that very precious Friendship and Good Will, with which she has hitherto honoured them; and with beseeching God to shower on Her the choicest Blessings, &c.

This is the Insolence, the Treachery, the Injustice, *&c.* the States have been Guilty of.

After

After having thus injuriously misrepresented the Conduct of the Allies, and the late M——y; he comes now to lay open *the real Causes of our present Misery. All this*, says he, *we were forc'd to submit to, because the General was made easy; because the Monied Men at Home were fond of the War; because the Whigs were not firmly settled; and because that Exorbitant Degree of Power, which was built upon a suppos'd necessity of employing particular Persons, wou'd go off in Peace.* After so full an Answer has been made, a very few words will serve to confute all these Calumnies. And first, the General was not made easy by the *Dutch*, as he seems to intimate; he never had any Present from them, nor any Annual Pay; no part in the Contributions; nor any Profits shar'd between him and the States; no Presents from any of our Allies for this five or six Campaigns; no Perquisites, but what have been allow'd to other Generals; nor any Stoppages from Subsidies, but what have been apply'd to the Service. He has in none of these Respects been made easy; but has rather been under great uneasiness often-times, to bring all the Parts of so great a Confederacy, into Right and Vigorous Measures. The Monied Men had no reason to be fond of the War: If the Interest of Money had been as great under the late Administration, as it was before, or has been since, there wou'd have been some Reason in what he says. They had but five *per Cent* for their Money almost all the whole time, which wou'd have turn'd to a much better Account, had it been employ'd in Trade, which the Opportunities of a good Peace wou'd have afforded them; This is so evident, that the rest he has to say on this Head, is not worth Answering.

Next, says he, *The Whigs were not firmly settled*: But how is this prov'd? Because the P——t in *December* 1707, humbly offer'd it to Her Majesty, as their Unanimous Opinion, *That no Peace cou'd be Safe or Honourable, if* Spain *or the* West-Indies, *or any Part of the* Spanish *Monarchy, were suffer'd to remain in the House of* Bourbon. And what was the occasion of this Vote? But because the M——y and the G——l having *refus'd to accept very Advantageous Offers of Peace, after the Battle of* Ramelies, *were forc'd to take in a set of Men, with a previous Bargain, to skreen them from the Consequences of that Miscarriage.* By this Account the Whigs were not taken in till the end of the Year 1707, and this Vote was to skreen the M——y, for refusing the Terms of Peace offer'd after the Battle of *Ramelies.* Now if they were not taken in till then, the rejecting those Offers do's not lye at their Door: Nor the Alliances with *Portugal* and *Savoy*, the Effect of Whig Councils; by which Treaties, the Restitution of the *Spanish* Monarchy to the House of *Austria*, is as strongly insisted on, as it cou'd be by the Vote of 1707. But the Account the Conducter gives of this Vote is utterly false; for it was not to skreen the M——y, or so much as oblige them by it; but on the contrary, 'twas to prevent what there was at that time no reason to fear, the clapping up an in-secure Peace, contrary to all our Alliances, and to what had been always the Sence of the Nation.

Nor did the M——y want to be skreen'd on that occasion, since what was offer'd was only the *Partition Treaty*, which if they had accepted, they wou'd have deserv'd an Impeachment as well as their Predecessors; and tho' it were never so false a step to reject these Offers, it had been much more to the Author's purpose to have dropt it, unless he cou'd have prov'd that the then Sec—— had disapprov'd it; which he was so far from doing, that there was not any one step taken in that Affair, which he was not acquainted with; nor any Answer made to the Offers of *France*, which were not consulted with him, and intirely approv'd by him. In short, both he and the late T——r, rejected those Offers, with the Indignity they deserv'd from every true *English* Man, and good Servant to the Queen. And if the Whigs were for continuing the

War,

War, it is plain it was not from any selfish Views, but meerly for the Good of their Country, and because *France* was not reduc'd to those Terms, which the Future Safety of *Europe* requir'd.

But in the last place, as to the late M———y, if they were so very blameable in their *Conduct*, let us see what the present M——y have done to Remedy the Abuses, complain'd of in their Predecessors? Have they reduc'd the Interest of Money? Or found out easier Methods of pursuing the War? Has the *South-Sea* paid the Publick Debts? Had not the Creditors rather have their Interest paid them without Trade? And are any considerable Funds provided for that Interest? Are not the Ways and Means for carrying on the War the very same they were before? Have they carried the Stress of the War into any more proper Place? Has the War in *Spain* been push'd with any more Vigour? Or rather has not less been done there this Year than ever? Has any thing been done in *Savoy*? Have we been able to act any where on the Offensive, but in *Flanders*? To which we owe most of our Successes, and from whence in the end we must expect a good and lasting Peace. In fine, have the New M———y done any thing that has given more Life to the War? Or toward redressing the General Complaint at Home? They have indeed made an Expedition to the *West-Indies*, which the late M——— y never attempted; but to what Account has it serv'd? Only to convince us that all such Schemes are *Visionary Prospects*, *and Romantick Views*: Were a bare Miscarriage is not the worst of it: 'Tis not only so much Money lost, but a weak'ning of our selves in other Parts, a Melancholy instance of which I have shewn already we have sufficiently felt, and shou'd not add any thing to what I've said, but as *One* is provok'd to it by the **Conducters** Incessant and Endless Abuses of the late M———y; we find here seven or eight Transports lost with twenty six Companies of Foot, and hardly a Man fav'd ; and the whole Fleet preserv'd only by a Miracle: And the Remains of these Troops, which might have been employ'd to the greatest Advantage elsewhere, brought Home again in a very Miserable Condition; and to compleat this great Misfortune, the Admiral's Ship blew up at *Spithead*, and in her, 'tis to be fear'd, a great part of the Stores, that can't be otherwise accounted for. Now all the use I desire to make of this, is, only in Vindication of the late M—— y, who seem to be so highly blam'd by the Conducter, for not carrying on a Naval War, and attempting something against the Enemy in the *West-Indies*, which by the Experience of this Expedition, (tho' I grant it to be well concerted) plainly appears, that such Schemes are Chymerical in themselves, and have only Specious outsides to delude unthinking People, who look no further than the bare View of things as they find them Represented ; and that 'tis in Effect proving that the Conduct of the late M———y is not to be excell'd by all the Endeavours that the Ablest and Wisest Men can use.

Of the five Reasons that the Conducter lays down for a hasty Peace, I have mention'd two of them, and now return to the third : Which is, *That our present Condition makes it impossible for us to carry on the War.* It would however have been as great an Argument of the Conducter's Zeal and Honour for his Country, as it is of his Abilities, had this Point been conceal'd ; for what can be of a more fatal Consequence in any Government, than to Dispirit, and Weaken the Hearts of the People ? And the Advantages and Encouragements we give the Enemy, even while a Peace is Transacting, and the Terms of it like to be Proportion'd, according to the Condition the Enemy think us in. Such a betraying of their Country, wou'd be suffer'd in no Nation under Heaven, but our own ; nor here neither, if it were not to serve a very wretched *Purpose*. Nothing of this is to be

found

found in *France*, and if it might be suffer'd there with Impunity, 'twou'd be hard to find a *French* Man so abandon'd to all Shame and Dishonour, as to be Guilty of so foul a Villainy, a Villainy that Robs the Crown of it's Greatest Support, the Spirit and Vigour of the People uniting chearfully in its Defence; and at the same time equally Encouraging the Enemy to start new Difficulties, and to refuse such Terms, as before they wou'd have submitted to in the Humblest and most Thankful manner; while their Disgraces and Misfortunes were much fewer than they are now, unless I may bring in some late Instances of Providence, by which Heaven seems to have taken the Work into its Hands, and to leave Mankind no more to do, no not even the Conducter himself, or the ablest and most exalted of his Friends. Our Allies by it are recovering their suprizes, and taking Heart, as fast as the Friends of *France* are losing Ground; and it seems impossible they shou'd prevail against us whilst we are under so Blessed a Protection.

But perhaps, says he, *our Allies will make up the Deficiency on our side, by greater Efforts of their own. Quite the contrary; both the Emperor and* Holland *fail'd last Year in several Articles; and signified to us sometime ago, that they cou'd not keep to the same Proportions in the next. We have gain'd a Noble Barrier for the latter, and they have nothing more to ask or desire. The Emperor, however Sanguine he may now affect to appear, will, I suppose be satisfied with* Naples, Sicily, Milan, *and his other Acquisitions, rather than Engage in a long hopeless War for the Recovery of* Spain, *to which his Allies the* Dutch, *will neither give their Assistance, nor Consent. So that since we have done their Business; since they have no further Service for our Arms, and we have no more Money to give them; and lastly, since we desire no Recompence, nor expect any Thanks, we ought in Pity to be dismiss'd, and have leave to shift for our selves.*

'Tis pity but the Conducter had been made Secretary to the Embassy; he had certainly sav'd the Congress an infinite deal of Labour. There had been no occasion to require a number of Days for adjusting Preliminaries; he has given them an unanswerable Scheme of Peace in fewer Minutes, and Couch'd in hardly so many Lines, as those in a Formal and Lingering way of a Treaty, are contain'd in Sheets of Paper: I wish I cou'd not affirm that there are more Notorious Falsities than either. *The Dutch and the Emperor let us know that they cou'd not keep up their Proportions.* And this we must believe, tho' it is so profuse a Lie, that both the Emperor and the States have teaz'd us with incessant Applications to be heard; and when they were heard, gave the fullest Assurances of doing all that we cou'd possibly require. And what is yet more (contrary to the Conducter's desire, I believe that it shou'd be so) we begin to be pretty sensible they are in earnest too; But when I say this, 'tis in hopes he has no new Difficulties to start in the behalf of his Friends in *France*. *We have Conquer'd a Noble Barrier for the* Dutch, *and they have no more to ask or desire.* False again as it happens: For we are convinc'd; and so may the Conducter too if he pleases to peruse their Demands, that they ask something more, and will go near to stand to it too, unless Providence favours his *Cause* more than it seems to have done of late. *The Emperor will accept of* Naples, Sicily, Milan, *and his other Acquisitions*, &c. What an unlucky thing is it now, that nothing but the whole *Spanish* Monarchy will please him. *To which his Allies the* Dutch, *will neither give their Assistance nor Consent.* 'Twas certainly a very unhappy Time when he was thus wasting his Judgment in Politicks that he so little understood, and arrogating to himself the Opinion of knowing more of the *Dutch*, than they know of themselves. And as to us, *We desire no Recompence, nor expect no Thanks, and therefore ought in Pity to be dismiss'd, and have leave to shift for our selves.* There's an End of the War at once; and plainly Represents

to

to us the Vanity of sending Plenipotentiaries to end it by a tedious and chargeable Treaty.

But if we do not hearken to Peace, others certainly will. Were this to be prov'd now it wou'd be something: But while it is only spoken upon bare Supposition, and by one who wou'd count it the happiest Event of his Life to be believ'd, I cannot see that any more heed ought to be given to it, than to the Vilest and most Groundless Assertion in his Book. This is what we have so often had in our Mouths during the War; and been so cautious of on all occasions; *That* France *wou'd seek to divide the Allies.* When these Jealousies are infus'd, and come to make an Impression once, 'tis dividing us with a Witness. And tho' *France* was never able to Effect this great Work, we have a set of People now, that are doing it for *Her.* What cou'd be said with a greater Air of Malice? That the farther it is from Fact, the more Villainous the Design appears; which is in effect incensing us to break Faith with our Allies, by Affirming, that if we don't, they will break Faith with us. I must confess it is probable enough they might have done so, had they foreseen what has since happen'd; cou'd they have perceiv'd how the Eighth Article of the Grand Alliance wou'd be observ'd; or how short liv'd another Treaty wou'd be, that as much concerns them.

After having expos'd our Weakness, and laid us fairly open to the Enemy, He comes to these Words, *That if the War lasts another Campaign, it will be impossible to find Funds for supplying it, without mortgaging the Malt-Tax, or some Method equally desperate.* This in reality were a sufficient Reason to induce us to think of Peace, if it were laid down, only upon open and apparent Views; and not made a necessity to Humour, or protect a *Party*, whose Grandeur and Continuance, seems to be rais'd and fix'd on this Foundation. 'Tis certain, a Campaign there must be, and the necessary Supplies are the greatest

greatest part of them Voted already; nor cou'd it ever be thought that a Treaty cou'd be fix'd time enough to prevent it: If so, why all this hast for Peace? The Extraordinary Expences of a Campaign, part of which must of Consequence be spent during the Treaty, and the remainder cou'd not have cost us much? Or were the Friends of *France* afraid, consonant to our former Successes, that we shou'd have struck some blow that might possibly have animated our Allies above the Contemptible Schemes we have seen erected; And convince our Friends at Home, that we were not under those terrible Disadvantages of making an *ill Peace*, as the Conductor and his *Party*, thought necessary for their *Purpose* to make 'em believe. At least, methinks it might make 'em some amends to have Experienc'd this under a G———l of their own, when they might have *crow'd on their own Dunghil*, and pick'd up Incidents enough to have justify'd a change in their Opinions afterwards. But Providence in this point has pretty well furnish'd them already, and the least we can look for now, is that they will make as good a Peace as they can, and not furnish the Enemy with Arguments to beat down the Market, or encourage 'em upon any Account, to trifle with our Allies: Since this is only requir'd of them; and this alone is sufficient to do our business, 'tis rather to be hoped, that they will drop the Conducter so far, as to throw in more vigorous Arguments, for a good and lasting Peace, than he has made use of.

But again, in the next Paragraph, he tells us; *That if Peace be made this Winter, we are to consider what Circumstances we shall be in towards paying a Debt of Fifty Millions? Which is a third part of the purchase of the whole Island were it to be sold.* To this I shall only add one short Remark, and leave the rest to the Conducter's own Meaning: There is a Consideration, which to me gradually falls in between these two Points. To Reflect well, if this be our

Case

Case what we shall do with another War, which a hasty Peace may subjugate us to in a few Years: People are now *in*, and tho' they struggle with some hardships, are in hopes that 'tis near an End, and that a lasting Peace will make 'em some amends: But shou'd another War break out in any little time, they wou'd be Heartless, Thunder-struck, and sink under the Melancholly Appehensions of being undone; no Care, no Consolation wou'd recover 'em: our Traders wou'd seek shelter in Forreign Climates, and our Young Men hide themselves in Holes and Desarts to avoid the Wars, of which they had heard such dreadful Tales; and of whose Events, no Man cou'd form any Judgment, without the utmost Reflection of Despair and Ruin. Therefore, I say, if our Debts are so hard to pay, and we shall Labour under so many Difficulties even in Peace; What Care, What more than ordinary Caution ought it to infuse into us, that the same be Safe, Lasting, and Honourable? Nay, that it ought to be put out of the hazzard of every thing, but the unforeseen Events of future Providence, since I must and will affirm it is within the Scope of Probability, if not a certainty, to bring it to pass.

But, says the **Conducter**, *To think that* Britain *must be ruin'd without the Restitution of* Spain, *is a strong delusion; as if Princes and Great Men cou'd find no way of settling the Publick Tranquility without changing the Possessions of Kingdoms.*

Whether it may be said, that *England* is ruin'd without the Restitution of *Spain*, I will not take upon me to say; it may be not: But I must venture to alledge, that it lays us under a very hazardous probability of it, which we ought to provide against; and farther, which we may as well provide against as not; by opposing the most violent and unjust Usurpation. And since they do not pretend to deny the undoubted Right of the House of *Austria*, will it not be a surer, as well as a juster way of setling *the Publick Tranquility?* Much rather than ruining a Great and Antient Monarchy, by parcelling it out to so many as is intended by this new Scheme, which *Europe* cannot possibly be long easy in. That the Recovery of *Spain* is not impracticable, or at least was not thought so eighteen Months ago, let the Enemies own Offers be Witness, when in the most solemn manner they consented to give it up entire; and will do so now, if their unseasonable Applications are rejected with that Scorn and Indignity, which in Justice and Honesty they heartily deserve. *But if the new Schemes*, says he, *are probable*, 'tis *enough*; *Probalities are cheaper by six Millions a Year.* But, as I have hinted before, we had better be at the Expence of twice six Millions for a certainty, than run the hazzard of paying so dear for a probability; where if we happen to be mistaken, which is not improbable, the Liberty both of us and our Allies, will be forfeited to the long dreaded Scheme of *Universal Monarchy.*

I come now to his Fourth Reason for Peace: Which is, *That the Condition of* France *is not so low, nor the Consequences of our Successes so great, as is commonly imagin'd.* They were of Consequence enough to humble a very haughty Enemy, some years ago, and if many repeated Successes since have render'd his Condition better, he is the more beholding to his *Friends.* From hence it is perhaps, that the Conducter affirms, *We might have had a better Peace two years ago than we can now, and that by a parity of Reason We must expect one so much worse two years hence.* Indeed if we have no more Success in our Undertakings, than we have had since the old M——y went off, 'tis very probable that by chance he has spoke Truth; which must be follow'd by another necessary Consequence by his Argument, That the longer the *New* continue, the worse Condition our Affairs will be in. I presume he wou'd have baited the

Compliment

Compliment to his Friends, out of the Antithesis of this worthy Proposition.

Have the Towns *France* has lost in this time made her Stronger? or has the continuance of the War made her Richer? or are we to suppose the nearer the Dangers approach to them, the more averse they are to Peace? So near, that one Defeat, nay one Siege wou'd lay their whole Kingdom open, even to their Capital. *But every Town we take*, he says, *costs us Fifty times more than 'tis worth.* If this be true, it ought to be remember'd, that 'tis the *Dutch* pay for it, and not *England.* This too, the Conducter might have left out; and I suppose, wou'd too, did not his Zeal sometimes, in the Cause he serves, make him run into oversights. It is much with the same Caution that he intimates it to the Advantage of the *French* King; *That his Money is spent in his own Country.* Which must needs be a mighty Consolation to him. Where besides the loss of the Revenue of many great Towns and Provinces taken from him, he is forc'd to suffer his Country to be ravag'd by his own Troops, as well as those of the Allies. His Subjects must needs be in a better Condition to pay their Taxes, and support the War, by paying large Contributions on the one side, and finding Forrage and Subsistence on the other, for two or three Hundred Thousand Men, all the Winter.

I am at length arriv'd to his last Reason for an inconsiderate and hasty Peace; which he gives us in the following Words: Lastly, *Those who are so violent against any Peace without* Spain *being restor'd to the House of* Austria, *have not, I believe, cast their Eye upon a Cloud gathering in the* North, *which we have help'd to raise, and may quickly break in a Storm upon our Heads.* What he means by

our

our helping to raise it, I don't understand: Instead of raising that Cloud, it is apparently known both the Qu—— and the States have been ever most Solicitous to prevent its gathering. But what he has said on this Head, if there be any meaning in it, he has himself answer'd, by telling us that *the Success of the War is various*; and so long as it is so, I see no great Injury in it to the *Confederate Cause*. *How if it shou'd break in any Storm upon our Heads*, is not easily to be understood; I hope we shall have no Reason to fear Alliances with *Infidels*. There is occasion, I confess, to suspect the Will of a certain Prince, if his Abilities at this time were answerable to his good Intentions. The *Confederate Cause* is indebted to him some considerable Obligations, the Emperor in particular; and notwithstanding the repeated Tergiversation we have been complimented with from that Quarter; I dare be positive, that when the matter shall be impartially enquir'd into, it will appear that we have done no more than the most Disinterested People in the World cou'd do: That both the *Dutch* and we, have labour'd with all the good Offices in our Powers to keep the Ballance even, and to have render'd the projected Neutrality of as much benefit to *Sweden*, as to any of the *Confederated Powers* at War with him. However, as to the Danger threaten'd to the *Common Cause*, from the War on that side; since the **Conducter** has mention'd it, I must say, I think we are not in any great hazard of being hurt by it; and before that time comes, it is very probable we may be at Leisure to retaliate Favours, by mediating Terms of Peace between those *Powers*, instead of receiving Terms from them.

And here, I leave the **Conducter**, having run thro' his Libel, with all the Care and Circumspection

ſpection I cou'd well promiſe my ſelf. And as I have had the Advantage of Reading others, who have writ excellently, tho' not *Fully*, on this Subject before me; whoſe Arguments perhaps for the greater Efficacy I have ſometimes follow'd; ſo I think I have left little more to be ſaid to him: The Reflection of his own Folly, Baſeneſs, and Malice, can only correct him farther.

FINIS.

[illegible]

FINIS.

www.ingramcontent.com/pod-product-compliance
Lightning Source LLC
LaVergne TN
LVHW012202040326
832903LV00003B/62